TO LOVE A MUSLIM!

TO LOVE
A MUSLIM!

by Edward F. Challen

GRACE PUBLICATIONS

Managing Editors — H. J. Appleby
— P. M. Misselbrook M.A. B.D.

GRACE PUBLICATIONS TRUST
139 Grosvenor Avenue
London N5 2NH
England

© Edward Challen 1988

Distributed by
EVANGELICAL PRESS
16/18 High Street
Welwyn
Hertfordshire   AL6 9EQ
England

ISBN 0 946462 15 1
British Library Cataloguing-in-Publication Data available

Typeset by Eurobooks, Welwyn
Printed in Great Britain by Cox & Wyman, Reading

CONTENTS

FOREWORD

For a long time I have felt that we conservative evangelical Christians are lacking both in our understanding and effectiveness in ministering God's word to those of the Muslim faith. For this reason alone I welcome this book and I am sure many of us will profit from reading its pages.

Having been involved from the beginning in the arranging of a conference to consider our involvement with Muslims I have been tremendously blessed. The day was one of great blessing to many who attended. Some friends have asked if the sessions could be put in print in order to have a permanent record. They also wanted something to place in the hands of folk who they feel would value such a presentation. This book is the answer.

If we are to fulfil our Lord's Great Commission to go into all the world and preach the gospel, to make disciples, and to baptise them in the name of the Father, Son and Holy Spirit, we need to begin where Muslims are. In order to do that we need to know what they believe.

It is my prayer that this book will have a wide circulation and that it will give us a burden to go and minister to those of the Muslim faith who are living on our doorsteps. Are we learning "To Love a Muslim"?

Colin Greenwood
Brentford
October 1986

PREFACE

The material contained in this book was first given as lectures under the title "Facing the Muslim: Are We?" on February 1st 1986. The author was invited to present them by the S.W. District of the Metropolitan Association of Strict Baptist Churches (now known as the Association of Grace Baptist Churches (South East)). A request was made that the lectures be produced in written form. In re-drafting the lecture notes the author has made a number of alterations and additions with the intention of making the book that much more beneficial to the reader.

This book, following the pattern of the lectures, is divided into two sections. Part I deals with the religion of Islam as it presents itself. In Part I comment on Muslim beliefs and understanding is intentionally avoided. It is all too easy to cloud the issues and to perpetuate misunderstanding. It is assumed that the reader is able to compare his own spiritual convictions with what he reads. Part II is devoted to an application of the gospel of the Lord Jesus Christ to the challenge posed in Part I. An attempt has been made to show how it is possible to take the gospel to the Muslim. The great need is not merely to acknowledge the opportunities, but to consider practical perspectives with respect to gospel witness. We need to overcome our ingrained sense of despair, and face the issues with a biblical understanding and with spiritual strength.

The author firmly upholds those standards of biblical truth that are commonly termed the Doctrines of Grace. There has been very little serious application of this theological outlook to both mission in general and, in particular, to the challenge that the religion of Islam brings to us. The author is firmly convinced that such a deficiency needs both to be recognised and adequately dealt with. Perhaps this publication may help many to face Islam with boldness and confidence from a position of spiritual strength and conviction by faith in the word of God.

Edward Challen
Epsom
May 1987

All Scripture quotations are from the New King James Version (Revised Authorised), published by Thomas Nelson, Inc., 1982.

At the request of the author, capitalisation in this book conforms to the conventions of the American edition of the above Scripture version.

PART ONE

THE MUSLIM WORLD

Part I.

Introduction

Even though we live in an enlightened age in so many outstanding ways, and knowledge is available to us on a scale never before experienced, it appears that with respect to the Muslim we are painfully ignorant. Many Christians in the western world know very little of what Islam stands for, or what it believes. Nor do they appear to care. This is a sad indictment against the Church, for it has received a commission to take the gospel to all people. In this cosmopolitan day in which we live, with immigrants from many nations appearing on our doorsteps, and living in our communities, we are finding that these people are coming to us. Are we as burdened to reach the unreached as we claim to be?

Sadly, a very deep-rooted intolerance of and resentment against the Muslim can be identified among Christians in this country. This attitude has been perpetuated through successive generations, and it could be claimed to be a hangover from the 12th century Crusades. The suspicion and bias is still maintained even through contemporary books on church history. This may be illustrated from a fairly recent review published as a one volume Church History written with the more general Christian reader in mind (as opposed to the scholar). I refer to it only to draw attention to the problem, and to show how easy it is to accept a view without discernment.*

> "When the church went astray. . . the Lord sent trials and
> afflictions to correct His unfaithful children. The greatest

* *The Italics are mine, indicating questionable statements.*

trial of all was connected with the person named. . . Mohammed. . . Mohammed was a *sickly child who suffered from epilepsy* and this undoubtedly influenced the whole course of his life. . . He . . . *formed the conviction that a new religion was needed* . . . and conceived the idea that he was a *messenger from God*. . . He gave his new religion the name Islam. . . He acknowledged that Moses and Jesus were prophets, but *claimed that he, Mohammed, was the greatest prophet of them all*. He said that Jesus was a holy man, but denied that he was the Son of God, for, he argued, God, being one, could not have a Son. He also *denied the virgin birth of Christ*, his resurrection and ascension. Never has the Christian faith had a greater enemy than Mohammed. . . Mohammedanism is the only world-religion established since the coming of our Lord Jesus Christ into the world, and it has remained the chief of all the enemies of Christianity. Converts from it to the Christian faith have invariably been few and hard-won."
(Houghton 1980: 34-38)

Sadly that quotation is a mixture of both truth and misinformed comment presented in a somewhat insensitive fashion. The title 'Mohammedanism' is a term of great offence to the Muslim, and we do not win either his respect or confidence by using it. In consequence it is perhaps not at all surprising to have read the following statement in a recent news item:

"Recently a delivery of 40 copies of Mr. S. M. Houghton's *Sketches From Church History*, destined for a bookshop in Malaysia, was held up by the Ministry of Home Affairs of Malaysia. This hold up (and possible destruction of the books) was followed by it being banned in Malaysia, on the grounds that the chapter on Islam was considered to be 'prejudicial to national interest'. An appeal to the Ministry was turned down."
('Banner of Truth', Nov. 1985: 14)

Does this not show a remarkable degree of indifference with respect to our responsibility to "preach the gospel to all the nations"? Compare this with the following quotation that is written with concern and a deeply burdened heart to reach Muslims for Christ.

> "Muhammad's father died before he [Muhammad] was born . . . Muhammad's mother also died young, when he was six years old. . . Muslims often stress the fact that he was an orphan and that he raised himself up from nothing, by his own efforts. . . Muhammad became accustomed to living very simply and as soon as he was old enough he began to work for his living. . . [At] the age of 40. . . Muhammad received his first revelation and message from God. It is said that he was greatly disturbed by it, not knowing whether it was from God, or from the Devil. . . It seems clear that Muhammad was already established as an upright, responsible person, able to give others advice and support, before his life was changed by the revelation of God calling him to be his messenger. Gradually those closest to him began to believe in his prophetic role. . ."
> (Cooper 1985: 77-78)

This is not a case of attempting to paint a better picture of the situation, but more of an honest attempt to discover what Muslims really do believe, so that we as Christians may be better equipped to present the glorious claims of Christ.

We may also look at the situation from another perspective. What does the Muslim see when he looks at us? Is he endeared to us as those who are willing to listen to his heartfelt needs with a measure of understanding? Or does he see us as a threat because of all that he misunderstands about us and our motives, let alone our faith? One missionary who works among these people records the following incident that took place in a restaurant in Washington, D.C., U.S.A.

"'*Why don't Christians follow the way of Jesus?*' a Muslim asked. I was dining with a close friend, a Muslim . . . when he leaned close and asked that disturbing question. He continued slowly, pensively, 'When I read the gospel, I am overjoyed. The life and teachings of Jesus are wonderful, wonderful, really, truly wonderful. But please, show me Christians who are willing to follow in the *sunna* (way) of Jesus.' We sipped our cardamon spiced tea in reflective silence, and then he continued. 'I have met a few, very few people who try to follow Jesus. But they follow him only in their private lives. Consequently your American society has becomes very evil. It seems to me that you Christians really do not believe that the *sunna* of Jesus is practical. That makes me very sad.'"

(Shenk 1983: 144)

This may sound rather unexpected, coming from a Muslim. Yet it is not a unique statement. We must not compromise our position as to the sovereign grace of God in order to win Muslims for Christ. We must rather be raising the standard of our personal spiritual life and witness, so that Muslims and others will notice the difference in us, and be drawn to Him whom we love because He first loved us.

It is intended by this book to highlight the general beliefs of Muslims, and to encourage a healthy respect for biblical truth. These are both necessary to our task of reaching Muslims for Christ.

1.
The Challenge of Islam

The history of the outworking of the Lord's commission to the Christian Church sadly demonstrates the fact that there has been very little meaningful contact with the world of Islam. There have been wonderful but exceptional occasions when godly men have been burdened for Muslim peoples. Such men as Henry Martyn and Samuel Zwemer have made a considerable impression on us, through their concern and dedication to a difficult and relatively unrewarding task.

It has to be said with deep regret that Muslim peoples have been a neglected mission field for far too long. This has been a tragedy for both the Church and Islam. Christians appear to have had very little to say to Muslims in any constructive sense. Great barriers of communication and an immense prejudice against Islam have been maintained for many a long year. The result has been that the task of presenting the gospel to Muslims has been a somewhat weak, apologetic, and almost non-existent affair in many places.

There is no doubt that the challenge of Islam is immense. Islam constitutes a formidable opponent to the Christian faith. The problem should be neither underestimated nor ignored. It must be admitted that historically the task has appeared to present so many difficulties that we have rather tended to formulate the word "impossible" in our minds, if not actually on our lips! Thus we turn away from the problem. Why is this so? It is our lack of faith, and this ought not to be the case.

As those who claim to believe in the great doctrines of the grace of God, are we not failing to apply them here? We say that we believe in the God who is sovereign in the exercise of His authority, wisdom and power over all peoples. We are surely to realise the implications of this truth and confidently assert that

"with God nothing will be impossible." Luke 1:37

Islam is an issue that clearly faces us today. It is right on our doorstep and will not go away. It claims our attention. What are we doing about it?

Ought we not to admit that the prospect of facing up to this problem engenders a certain amount of fear in the hearts of many Christians? We would far rather turn our backs on this question: to act as if it does not really exist. We are tempted to feel that it is easier to ignore it, rather than to face up to its challenge.

Yet, to do so would surely diminish the importance of our missionary mandate, and our responsibility to it. We would be undermining the explicit command given us by the Lord himself; that we are to

"Go into all the world and preach the gospel to every creature."   Mark 16:15

To ignore the challenge of Islam is to admit that we who are Bible-believing Christians doubt God's sovereign power as King of kings and Lord of lords. God's word plainly tells us that the Lord Jesus Christ faced the full wrath of God against all sin and all forms of rebellion against His majesty. He met the full force of the power of Satan and fully overpowered him. The Son of God Himself overcame *all* the effects of sin; *all* the power of Satan. *Every* power that can be named was trodden under His feet. The Lord Jesus Christ *is* victorious. He is the sovereign Lord, the Redeemer and only Saviour. It is on the basis of His triumphal conquest, His glorious work of redemption, that Christ himself now commissions us who believe. What He has effected in principle we, by His saving grace, are to work out in practice. His conquest of the power of Satan is an accomplished eternal fact that is still being applied in space and time, through the powerful administrations of His Holy Spirit, according to His glorious will and purposes, and the outworking of his grace.

The very words of our commission are important:

> **"All authority has been given to Me in heaven and on earth."**   Matthew 28:18

Here Christ's own personal declaration of His sovereign power is all the more gloriously expressed because of His completed work of salvation. As Paul asserted, the Lord is now

> **"declared to be the Son of God with power, according to the Spirit of holiness, by the resurrection from the dead."**   Romans 1:4

It is important to notice that Paul goes on to speak emphatically about the effect that Christ's demonstration of power brings. It is through Him that

> **". . . we have received grace and apostleship for obedience to the faith among all nations for His name."**   Romans 1:5

The apostle Paul continues to give us a further encouragement, a real stimulus to obedience:

> **". . . among whom you also are the called of Jesus Christ."**   Romans 1:6

This same power is available to us. In our context we may make this particular, and I believe, legitimate application: that if *we* have been called by His grace, there is then no reason why He cannot call our Muslim brothers also, for we all are sinners who may be called by His grace. The Lord sovereignly calls out His Church. *He* builds His Church. The gates of hell, He has promised, shall not prevail against it.

We need to affirm that we believe the gospel: for then there remains no obstacle to faith that cannot be surmounted. The gospel is the word of God, and He has promised that His word will not return to Him void, that is, prove ineffective and without results. After his great affirmation of his belief in the power and sovereignty of Christ, Paul was able to say,

> **"I am not ashamed of the gospel of Christ, for it is the power of God to salvation for everyone who believes."**   Romans 1:16

Paul then adds the reason for his being so convinced, drawing from the evidence of the gospel itself:

> **"For in it the righteousness of God is revealed from faith to faith; as it is written, 'The just shall live by faith.'"**   Romans 1:17

Here immediately we have an encouragement to take the gospel to the Muslim and say, "You claim to be righteous by what you *do*. We know that true righteousness — the righteousness of God — which you sincerely seek, is only to be found through faith in the Lord Jesus Christ. God has clearly said this Himself in His revealed word. Believe His word for your salvation."

Furthermore, the hope that is set before us gives missionary vision and encouragement. We have been granted the privilege to share in that great vision which the apostle John was given in which he saw the Saviour, the slain Lamb of God, reigning in heaven and exercising His divine sovereign authority over every creature:

> **"I looked, and behold, a great multitude which no one could number, of all nations, tribes, peoples, and tongues, standing before the throne and before the Lamb, clothed in white robes, with palm branches in their hands, and crying**

> out with a loud voice, saying, 'Salvation be-
> longs to our God, who sits on the throne, and to
> the Lamb.'"
>
> Revelation 7:9-10

Who are the people John sees so vividly? The answer is given by him in these words:

> **"These are the ones who come out of the great
> tribulation, and washed their robes and made
> them white in the blood of the Lamb."**
>
> Revelation 7:14

Here a glorious assurance is given to us that even those from a Muslim background will have believed the gospel. No people who live on earth is to be excluded from the privileges of hearing and receiving the gospel message. Even those who once were Muslims will be standing before the throne and praising God. They will have come to know Christ's saving grace. They too will be privileged to wear those white robes of righteousness before His throne in heaven, together with us.

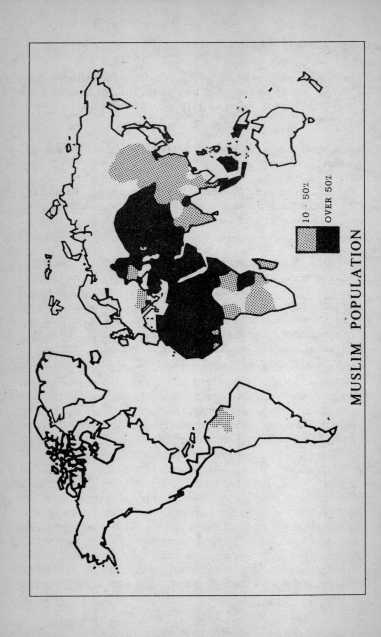

MUSLIM POPULATION

10 - 50%

OVER 50%

2.
The World of Islam

Islam was like a great earthquake that shook the world from the 7th century on. Its epicentre was Mecca in Saudi Arabia, considered by Muslims, quite seriously, to be the centre of the world. The shock waves of Islam have been felt by the world ever since.

Islam began in the two holy cities of Mecca and Medina through Mohammed's puritanic reaction to the decadence and social problems among the Arabs of his day. History books tell us of the way Arabs associated themselves with him during his lifetime: how they took Mecca by force and established it as the Holy City; of their speedy conquests by the sword that took place after his death, as well as in his lifetime; of the internal bickering and argument that splintered the 'one brotherhood' into many factions. Interestingly, there is a tradition that Mohammed himself is alleged to have said *"My community will divide into seventy-three sects of which only one is correct"*. In fact Islamic history has produced vastly more sectarian groupings than that traditional number. Muslims have been no less fruitful than other religious communities in multiplying internal divisions!

From Saudi Arabia, Islam spread west into North Africa and up into Spain. It spread throughout the Middle East, through Palestine, up into Turkey and into central Europe, now the southern part of the USSR. It spread through Persia and Afghanistan into many parts of India. It travelled via trade routes reaching into China, Thailand, Malaysia, across into Indonesia, and up into the Philippines. In modern times its message has crossed the Sahara desert and is now to be found in many central African countries. Through immigration there are now some 6 million Muslims who have settled in European countries. We have some 1.5 to 2 million here in the United Kingdom, who have come from Pakistan, India, Bangladesh, together with an influential business population from Middle East countries. In the United States Muslims are the third largest religious group with some 2.5 million adherents.

We are therefore talking of about 850 million people, some 1 in 5 of the world population. Muslims are not insignificant. The countries with the greatest Muslim population are Indonesia (130 million), Bangladesh (100 million) and Pakistan (90 million), constituting together nearly 40% of the Muslim world population.

Islamic numerical strength is growing substantially, but it must be borne in mind that this is overwhelmingly due to a biological increase. There has been comparatively little growth by proselytisation. This situation may well be changing in the light of recent developments in Western countries. During the past 20 years Middle Eastern Muslim countries have been pleased to realise that they have control over substantial amounts of the world's oil reserves. This has given them a new sense of power, and a new sense of control over many world economies. We have to understand that this awareness of economic power has gone hand in hand with a resurgence of a far more militant, fundamental form of Islam than has been seen for many a long day. Together with this, there has been a strengthening presence of Muslims in the West through immigration from the Indian sub-continent, plus exiled and refugee Iranians, as well as large numbers of Middle East students and businessmen. Many of these Muslims are actively seeking to infiltrate western society by making their presence felt in the realms of education and politics, pressing, at the very minimum, for accommodation to their views, beliefs and values.

It cannot be questioned that the world of Islam has been having a significant impact on recent history. There has been a resurgence of religious fanaticism, as witnessed in Iran and Libya. Other countries in the Middle East and Asia have consolidated the place of Islam within their culture.

Where did it all begin? To answer this, and to understand something more of the character of Islam, we need to look at the life and circumstances of Mohammed, the prophet of Islam.

Mohammed was born at Mecca in the year A.D. 570. His father's tribe was that of the Quraysh, who had strong claims to being direct descendants of Ishmael. Mohammed's father died before Mohammed was born, and he was orphaned by his mother's death when he was only six years of age. He was subsequently brought up in somewhat unfortunate and difficult circumstances by his uncle, Abu Talib. When he was old enough to work, the wealthy widow Khadija employed him, eventually putting him in charge of her camel caravans. Later, when he was 25 years old, she rewarded him for his fidelity and competence by marrying him! As he carried out his duties he was constantly coming into contact with both Jews and Christians, though the latter, very sadly, were unorthodox Syrian Nestorians and Monophysites.*

Through his marriage Mohammed became a person of some considerable influence among his fellow countrymen, earning a measure of respect. As a result he was able to leave his business at times to those under his authority, so finding time for serious meditation. It appears that he was no infidel, nor did he act in any underhand way. He was well-liked and courteous; he was both eloquent and correct in his use of language; he was firm and

---

* *Both Nestorians and Monophysites held unorthodox views concerning the person of the Lord Jesus Christ. Neither group could understand how Christ could be both fully human and fully divine — two natures in one person. The Nestorians held that there were two separate persons in the incarnate Christ, the divine and human persons remaining distinct: they could not affirm the divinity of the man Christ Jesus. The Monophysites went to the opposite extreme of affirming that the incarnate Christ had only one nature, namely the divine. Their views undermined the true humanity of Christ.*

prompt in making decisions; and he was considered very faithful and generous to his workers, followers and friends. When he was about forty years of age he became deeply disturbed and troubled about religious issues, through considering the general attitudes of his people and their way of life. He began to retire frequently to a cave on the slopes of Mount Hira, some three miles from Mecca, a place that was known particularly for its barrenness and dreary outlook.

The Arabs at this time, he noted, were very superstitious and idolatrous, worshipping heavenly bodies and stones, particularly venerating a black stone in the Ka'aba (a temple in Mecca). Mohammed was troubled about the way they lived and behaved; many around him were living loose moral lives, drinking heavily and gambling to excess. These things had a profound effect on him. Mohammed's development of Islam should be understood in terms of a reaction to the idolatry and excesses of his day.

During his meditations Mohammed experienced trances, and an external power appeared to take hold of him. He found that he was enabled to find expression in eloquent and forceful language. On one particular occasion he saw what he described as a vision of the angel Gabriel who commanded him to recite certain passages. At first he refused, but eventually complied. Thus he learnt passages which he then recited to family and friends. The first message that he claimed was transmitted to him was this:

> "Recite in the name of your Lord who created, created man from drops of blood.
> Recite! Your Lord is the Most Bountiful One, who by the pen taught man what he did not know."
>
> (Qur'an: Sura 96:1-2)

Mohammed continued to have visions, and the complete record of what are claimed to be his revelations now comprises the book that is known as the *Qur'an*, meaning 'recital'.

The resulting history of how Mohammed took Mecca from

those he considered unbelievers and idolaters, and all the subsequent records, much of which we would consider very unsavoury and bloodthirsty, can be read from the various histories available (see bibliography). Much of the way that we see Muslims conduct themselves in some parts of the world today can be traced to the attitudes and actions of both Mohammed and his early followers. Some of it, however, must be understood not only in the light of Muslim teaching and attitudes, but also as a reflection of the temperament and culture of those who live in Middle Eastern countries.

The Muslim world is certainly complex. Many fixed attitudes and prejudices must be faced if we are going to undertake the task of presenting our gospel message seriously. There are indeed many problems that must be dealt with; but we will get nowhere if we do not apply ourselves in a serious attempt to understand the people who call themselves Muslims.

3.
Who Are The Muslims?

We may begin to answer this question by describing them as members of a community of people who hold to a system of religious teaching called *'Islam'*. The Word *Muslim* is an Arabic word, being the adjectival form of the noun *Islam*. *Islam* means 'submission': the surrendering of the complete person to God. It also carries the idea that one must accept God's will and be obedient to it.

Muslims consider that Islam is concerned with the direction provided by God for all mankind. Its principles guide and govern every aspect of individual and corporate living. Though the word itself does not mean 'peace', 'Islam' carries that connotation because this is the anticipated and assumed result of being totally surrendered to the law of God.

Islam is not seen as merely a religion, but rather a complete way of life. Muslims do not accept that Islam is one religion among many, but maintain that it is the only religion. The Qur'an states:

"The true religion with God is Islam."
(Qur'an: Sura 3:17 (Arberry))

Islam is a doctrine with universal application. Adam is considered to be the first Muslim. It is believed that the core message of the prophets and the messengers, from Adam through to Mohammed, is the same, i.e. obedience to God alone and submission to his law. The earlier messages had been sent to certain people only, and with time they had become distorted. Therefore Islam as revealed through the Qur'an and the exemplary role of

Mohammed's life is understood to be the one universal and final religion, for it is the perfection of all that God originally meant religion to be. One Muslim author has stated it thus:

> "Ours is a law-governed universe and everything in it is following the course that has been ordained for it . . . As the whole of creation obeys the law of God, the whole universe, therefore, literally follows the religion of Islam — for Islam signifies nothing but obedience and submission to Allah, the Lord of the universe . . . Everything in the universe is 'Muslim' for it obeys God by submission to His laws. Even a man who refuses to believe in God, or offers his worship to someone other than Allah, has necessarily to be a 'Muslim' as far as his existence is concerned."   (Mawdudi 1981:18)

This statement is noticeably all-inclusive and for this reason Muslims never consider themselves as persons having individual responsibility. First and foremost they are members of a brotherhood, a worldwide community of believers, who co-operate together in living for the glory of God. All that a Muslim does, he does corporately with other Muslims, and he will point to the testimony of the Qur'an:

> "Cling (hold fast) one and all to the faith of Allah and let nothing divide you. Remember the favours He has bestowed upon you: how He united your hearts when you you were enemies, so that you are now brothers through His grace; and how He delivered you from the abyss of fire when you were on the brink of it. Thus Allah makes plain to you His revelations, so that you may be rightly guided."
> (Qur'an: Sura 3:103-105)

Muslims point with pride to the fact that their scriptures testify that they are the "*best community*". That same verse also gives a reason:

> "You enjoin justice and forbid evil. You believe in
> Allah."   (Qur'an: Sura 3:110)

The three qualifications given, namely, (i) correct conduct
and right attitude, (ii) the forbidding of indecency, and (iii) the
belief in Allah, establish the faithful as Muslims. This set of
criteria is not often referred to by Muslims, but the Qur'anic
statement stands as a sociological reality which has the effect of
bonding Muslims together in a sort of mystical *ummah*, that is,
community. Muslims consider that the links of this community
are sealed for ever and they cannot conceive of them being
broken. Knowing this, one can begin to understand the tremendous clash that occurs when a Muslim dares to break the strands
of this community by becoming a Christian. The action is a direct
challenge to the very basis of Islam, not a mere ripple of the *status
quo*. The commands of the Qur'an invoke a keen sense of
responsibility to the community and a fear of breaking its bonds.

The concept of *ummah* is very important to Muslims who
believe that their community has been raised up for the the good
of mankind. It is in itself a model of righteousness. Therefore it
is not only unforgivable when someone attempts to break away
from it, but also utterly beyond belief. That anyone could ever
think of doing so is absolutely incomprehensible to the Muslim
mind!

The idea of community is based on the consideration that
God is the master Designer and Creator of the human race. He has
formed people into social structures. God's purpose is clearly
defined as creating a society in which all may come to recognise
each other and have a sense of belonging. As it is expressed in
the Qur'an:

> "Men, We [the plural is used of Allah to denote great
> honour and respect] have created you from a male and a
> female and divided you into nations and tribes that you
> might get to know one another. The noblest of you in

Allah's sight is he who fears Him most."
(Qur'an: Sura 49:13)

The ideal community is one composed of people who care for each other, as well as those who believe in God and the Prophet.

"Therefore, every one of the community is considered as a brother unto every other and this has found expression in the sayings of the Prophet (peace and blessing of Allah be upon him) who speaks of each member as a brother unto the other and enjoins him to wish for his brother what he wishes for himself."   (Muslehuddin 1977:231)

Thus Muslims tenaciously hold to the idea of community as a loosely knit brotherhood, very much like that which is described for us in 1 Corinthians 12, where Christians are portrayed as members of *one* body or community, different members having different gifts. The comparison is not absolute: we as Christians emphasise that we are building a spiritual house (1 Peter 2: 5), the spiritual body of Christ that has a physical expression in the practical fellowship of local churches. This is different from the Islamic outlook that looks for the physical identity and social expression of unity of belief as expressed by community.

The *Hadith* (Book of Traditions of Islam) adds another dimension to the idea of community: that of deploring racial prejudice with an insistence on the primary importance of piety. The whole of mankind is to be embraced without any distinction regarding colour or cultural differences. No difference can be recognised among the races as they pray together before the one God (it does not always work in practice, but that is the principle).

What is the cement that holds this community together and how may we identify it? It is the *bond of faith* that must be seen as the integrating force behind the movement. This is the stimulus that brings together tribes and nations that are seemingly poles apart in every other way. Islam is one of the most theocentric religions of the world, for God is totally central to all the activity of the faithful. Muslims are *not* worshippers of Mohammed, but only of God, believing that the prophet Mohammed was merely the favoured vehicle of God's final revelation to mankind. To the Muslim, faith is the practical application of the principles of Islam to everyday life. It is expressed by commitment to those principles (see chapter 4) and by a meticulous observance of the legal requirements. It is an explicit trust, not in a person (as for the Christian), but in a system, with the unassured hope that dedicated practice may merit God's approval and acceptance for Paradise. The Muslim considers this to be a 'saving faith', in that commitment and obedience expressed in good works is faith in practice. They believe that such faith must merit salvation (understood not as forgiveness of sins, but as one's good deeds outweighing one's bad deeds).

An important question we must ask is, 'How does this faith express itself in practice?' One commentary answers it in this way:

> "Islamic Law governs (more or less) the worship, the belief, the customs, the trade, and even the politics. Everyone adopts a certain style of politeness and cleanliness, everyone has an Arabic name, everyone joins in the fast and festivals, and often everyone wears the same style of clothes: all these things show the solidarity of the community."
> (Christian Witness 1971: 78)

This concept of solidarity is very important to grasp. It is the essence of Islam and pervades every aspect of life, so that the identity of an individual is always a secondary issue (if indeed it is ever considered!). This concept, above all the other teachings of Islam, represents the greatest challenge to us in winning Muslims for Christ. Providentially, we find through observation and experience that there is great inconsistency in the practice of Islam. Yet there is no room for complacency. If we are to face up to Islam, then we must recognise the formidable presence of its community spirit.

4.
The Expressions of Community

The practical manifestations of this community that make it unique are found in the summary of Muslim doctrinal practice known as the *"Pillars of Islam"*. These are five mandatory demands or statutory obligations placed upon every Muslim believer. In Islam, works are considered to be the expression of faith, faith being identified through various acts. For this reason, great emphàsis is placed upon these practices. They are themselves strictly governed by detailed regulations. The five specific duties are detailed in the Qur'an, and all the elaborate rules, or laws, are laid down in, and extracted from, the large body of Traditions. These Traditions are the *hadith*: recorded oral reports that have been passed on by contemporaries of the prophet Mohammed, describing various aspects of his life and thought.

i. *The Shahada*: the Confession, or Witness. This is reputedly the shortest creed in the world! It is certainly repeated more than any other. It is composed of a mere 8 words in Arabic.

> "There is no god but God (Allah), and Mohammed is the Apostle (Messenger/Prophet) of God."

This is repeated in Arabic by Muslims in their prayers and at countless other times in the day. It is used as a battle cry, and as an exclamation of joy at the birth of a baby. It is whispered into the ear at death, and heard as an incessant dirge at a funeral. Its recital is the means of becoming a Muslim — by repeating these words in Arabic in front of a judge, or two public witnesses. It is thus the method of admission to the community.

ii. *Prayer, Salat*: Before prayer can be performed, a Muslim
must be ceremonially clean; so he first washes in the prescribed
way. Here is at least a recognition that he is coming before a holy
God. He then has to pray a prayer of intention, to recognise the
need to apply both mind and heart to the intended purpose before
such activity can be meaningful or meritorious. This is also the
case before each statutory duty is performed.

Prayers are conducted barefoot on a clean floor or rug and
consist of a set cycle of words and ritual gestures (each cycle
being known as a *raka'h*). The number of cycles completed
depends on which prayer of the day it is. A Muslim is called to
prayer five times a day: at dawn, soon after mid-day, two hours
before sunset, immediately after sunset, and two hours after
sunset. The call to prayer, the *Adhan*, goes out from the mosque
to remind the faithful that "*God is most great*". It incorporates the
witness, the Shahada, and the dawn call includes the injunction
that "*prayer is better than sleep*". Prayer is always performed
towards Mecca, corporately, with theoretically no distinction of
class. It is proudly claimed that the beggar stands shoulder-to-
shoulder with the respectable classes.

Prayer engenders oneness in and identity with the community. It is the expression of the unity of the faith, of the purpose
of Islam, and a public declaration of the community itself.

iii. *Almsgiving, Zakat*: In practice this takes the form of a
compulsory payment, and is not charity. It is a levy of some 2.5%
on the possession of certain categories of property, rather than on
income. The proceeds are normally collected at the mosque, to
be distributed to the poor, usually on Fridays. True free-will
almsgiving is also encouraged over and above this statutory
requirement.

Incidentally, all property is considered to be on loan from
God and not 'personal property'. Owning property is therefore
considered a privilege and a trust, and all material possessions are
to be used for God's purposes among the community. The
concept of the self-possession of goods is considered a 'sin'

against (or perhaps affront to) both God and the community.*

Here we see the community concern evidenced. *Zakat* tangibly expresses the sense of responsibility that Muslims ought to have to one another, and especially to the less fortunate within the community.

iv. *Fasting, Sawm:* This is an obligation to be honoured on several specific occasions, the most important being the celebrated month of *Ramadan*, the ninth month of the Muslim lunar calendar, when, it is believed, the gates of Paradise are open, and those of hell are closed. All who fast meticulously will be pardoned for their past venial, i.e., excusable, sins. This is also the month during which the Qur'an is believed to have been revealed to the prophet Mohammed.

Muslim fasting is a very rigorous and demanding exercise. During the hours between sunrise and sunset nothing is to enter the body. The faithful are expected to spend as much time as possible in prayer, preferably at the mosque. The fast is broken at night, as soon as 'a white thread becomes indistinguishable from a black one', and a 'break-fast' snack is taken. Later in the evening a large meal is consumed, if it can be afforded. This is often a most sumptuous affair, that more than makes up for what would normally be eaten during the day. Another meal is prepared at night, which is to be consumed about an hour before sunrise.

No-one is actually exempted from taking part in the fasts, but the sick, travellers, pregnant women, nursing mothers, etc., are permitted to delay it to a more convenient time.

Incidentally, it is worth noting that Muslim lunar months

* In our experience of a Muslim country this was vividly portrayed. For example, one had to take care not to admire a certain ornament on visiting a Muslim family or one was likely to have to come away with it, to one's personal embarrassment! This shows the reality of the principle, as well as their natural generosity.

begin with the first sighting of the moon after a new moon. There
is therefore a certain amount of ambiguity regarding the start and
finish of Muslim months. When the young moon is first sighted,
a new Muslim month commences. When this happens at the
close of the month of Ramadan (ratified by a moon-sighting
committee!) there is a great celebration: that of *Id-ul-Fitr*. It is a
wonderful day of great rejoicing and feasting, and new clothes are
often given to the children as presents. This festival is an
expression of thanksgiving by the community for all God's
blessings, especially for those obtained through the great fast.
The fast itself is the collective recognition by the community of
their utter dependence on God for every blessing, and an expression of a deep desire for personal forgiveness.

v. *The Pilgrimage, Hajj*. The annual pilgrimage to the holy
city of Mecca is the largest multinational gathering of people on
earth. There may be around 3 million people who gather, and they
represent almost every ethnic group, political entity, economic
strata and skin colour known to the human race.

If financially feasible, every Muslim must make this Mecca
pilgrimage at least once in a life-time (more often if possible).
This is the goal and aspiration of all Muslims worldwide. Mecca
is uniquely the Islamic holy centre. No non-Muslims are allowed
within the city walls; immediate death is the penalty for breaking
this sacred rule. This prohibition itself strengthens the concept of
Muslim community.

The pilgrimage takes place in the 12th Muslim month, and
every pilgrim has to be in a prepared state of ritual consecration.
Each Muslim pilgrim shaves his head, washes completely, and
subsequently wears two plain seamless white sheets of cloth,
which leave only his head and face uncovered. Each pilgrim is
then to make seven walking circuits of the *Ka'aba*, kissing the
black meteorite stone. Each one is then to run between two small
hills outside the mosque, in imitation of Hagar's desperate search
for drinking water to give to Ishmael. On the 8th day of the month,
the pilgrims travel a distance of some twelve miles to Arafat,

where, next day, they assemble themselves from noon to sunset in prayer and meditation. The 10th day is the day on which Muslims everywhere, together with those on pilgrimage, sacrifice an appropriate animal to commemorate the joyful sacrifice of the animal that God gave in place of Abraham's son. Also on this day the pilgrims, at Mina, hurl stones at each of three rock pillars. This is believed to re-enact the scene when Abraham's son hurled stones at Satan in his terror, when he was expecting to be sacrificed.

The pilgrimage itself is the focus of the realised hope of the community. Every *Hajji*, as the pilgrim is known, believes that his total act of dedication in pilgrimage is the supreme means of obtaining the forgiveness of sins. Among the traditions there is one which says that every step taken by the pilgrim in the direction of the Ka'aba blots out a sin, and one who dies on this pilgrimage is enrolled among the martyrs and goes straight to heaven (this is why those Muslims with few means available to them often wait till they are much older before they undertake this pilgrimage). The Muslims' worldwide act of sacrifice at this time is considered to demonstrate: (i) the debt that the whole community owes to God, (ii) that Islam exhibits a remarkable solidarity of belief, and (iii) that the pilgrimage is itself a communal act of dedication to God. Though it is not officially considered to be a sacrifice for sin, or a means of redemption, experience appears to reveal that it is commonly thought to be so in practice.

The following statement is an invaluable insight into this remarkable affirmation of the Muslim's singleness of mind and purpose. It is one Muslim's personal view of the sense of Islamic community spirit shown in the pilgrimage.

"The social significance of the Hajj is a glorious testimony of the social equality and universal brotherhood of Islam. Dressed in two white pieces of cloth men and women of different countries of the Muslim world; irrespective of rich and poor; high and low; assemble together at Ka'aba testifying to their very presence there and to the unity of

Allah and also glorifying Him and expressing their grati-
tude in Him in the same breath at the top of their voices.
They stand shoulder to shoulder as no distinction exists
between the rich and poor, high and low. They are all
humble creatures of Allah forming one fraternity of true
believers and having the common idea of the same
Prophet. Such a spectacle of social equality and brotherhood is nowhere to be seen in the world." (Karim 1982)

5.
The Faith of The Community

We now come to consider what binds the Muslim community together. If we think of the "Pillars of Wisdom" as the foundation blocks of the Muslim community, then their Articles of Faith are the cement that holds them together.

i. *Belief in One God:* 'Allah' is the Arabic word that translates our English word 'God'. To the Muslim it is indicative of His essential being. We ought to take care not to think of Allah as the Muslim 'god' in opposition to what we believe about God as Christians. Etymologically, *Allah* is equivalent to the Hebrew *Elohim*, having common linguistic roots. The English term 'God' and the Arabic word 'Allah' are therefore synonymous. However, it is with the Muslim *understanding of who God is* that we have to take care. Islam does not accept the same revelation of God as we do. There is nevertheless some common ground.

Allah is recognised as the sovereign God, Creator of the universe: the sustainer and keeper of His creation. To a Muslim, the most important aspect of the truth about God is that He is one (*tauhid*): one in essence, not composed of parts; one in His attributes, not having a multiplicity of powers or will; one in His works, no other being besides God has any influence upon Him. One chapter of the Qur'an powerfully expresses this idea of the unity of God:

> "In the name of God, the Merciful, the Compassionate
> Say: 'God is One, the Eternal God.
> He begot none, nor was He begotten.
> None is equal to Him'." (Qur'an: Sura 112)

He has many attributes, and these are accorded to Him as names. Each of them is to be found in the Qur'an: ninety-nine in all (see Appendix 1). The hundredth name, for completion, is only known to God himself! We may note that many of these attributes are to be found in our Christian Scriptures also. There is, however, one significant name that is missing, i.e., "God is Love". In Islam, God is called "the loving One", but the term is understood to be a characteristic of the divine will, rather than an aspect of His nature.

Out of all Allah's attributes, there are seven which are considered principal. They are fundamental to the expression of his being.

a. *Life*: He is without beginning and without end: eternal.

b. *Knowledge*: He knows all things, never forgetting, never negligent, never making an error.

c. *Power*: He is almighty, able to do all things. His power can never diminish; it is as everlasting as He is.

d. *Will*: He is able to do whatever He wills: making believers, or unbelievers, according to His will.

e. *Hearing*: He can hear any sound, high or low, without ears.

f. *Seeing*:   He is able to see all things without eyes, even the steps of a black cat on a black stone on a black night.

g. *Speaking*:   He speaks, without a tongue.

It is worth noting that the description of these aspects of God's nature is a rather hesitant anthropomorphism! The Muslim views God as so very unlike His creation that nothing in creation may be associated with Him in any way. Therefore the Muslim theologian, to be able to relate who God is, and make Him understandable to the human mind, has to resort to this somewhat hesitant use of human parallels. Muslims are very fearful of applying such concepts to God in a too hard and fast way.

Three other important aspects of God must be stressed, for they are ever in the Muslim mind:

a. *"God is Great"* (*Allahu Akbah*):   This expression is constantly to be found on Muslim lips. It indicates that whatever a man may possibly think, or whatever idea he may hold with respect to God himself, by definition, God must be much greater.

b. He is a *Revealer* of His Will: His revelation of Himself and His will is the *Qur'an*, but only in the Arabic original (for Arabic is the language of heaven!).

c. He is *Transcendent*: He is not knowable in reality and can never be known by man. God is so very different from whatever man can think about Him.

ii. *Belief in Angels*: The doctrine of angels is a very comprehensive one. Muslims consider and teach that angels worship God continually and obey all His commands. It is said that the food of angels is celebrating God's glory, their drink is proclaiming God's holiness, their conversation is commemorating God and their pleasure is worshipping God. According to the Muslim idea of creation, angels were made from light, the devil from fire, and men from clay! Angels hold a position of respect that is slightly inferior to human prophets, on the basis that they were, according to the Qur'an, commanded to prostrate themselves before Adam (Qur'an: Sura 2:32). With respect to mankind, it is said that every believer is attended by two recording angels, one sitting on his right shoulder recording his good deeds, while the other is on his left shoulder recording his evil deeds. There is a definite order of angels, with an hierarchy of archangels who have specific responsibilities: *Jibra'il* (Gabriel) is the angel of revelation; *Mika'il* (Michael) the patron, or friend and protector of the Jews; *Israfil*, who is to sound the trumpet on the Last Day; and *Azra'il*, the angel of death. There is another angel, *Malik*, whose responsibility it is to supervise hell, and who has nineteen subordinates to assist him to do so. Another two, *Munkar* and *Nakir*, examine the dead in their graves on the night after their burial (or immediately after the funeral is over), to discover what they believe about God and Mohammed, and to torture them if they do not give satisfactory answers! The throne of God is supported by eight angels; others intercede on behalf of man and celebrate the praises of Allah. In general, it is believed that angels act as guardians to man. There is thus quite a complex understanding of angels.

We might also mention the *Jinn*. These are essentially evil spirits, though they are not necessarily antagonistic to men and women. They may be appeased. However, Muslims are very wary of them, and do anything and everything to avoid antagonising them, or attracting their attention. There is in fact an inbuilt, but little spoken of, fear of them. A great deal of folk superstition has consequently arisen around this particular belief, much of which can be identified as animistic.

Tradition also colours their doctrine of the devil. He is known as *Shaitan* or *Iblis*, and is the father of all the jinn. He can enter a man's body and be just as the blood that flows in him. Not only does the Muslim believe that he has an angel guarding him, but also that there is a devil (demon) appointed over him. Every child of Adam, except Jesus and Mary, is touched by the devil at his birth and this causes the new-born infant to cry!

iii. *Belief in the Books of God*: Every Muslim is to believe in the divinely inspired books which God has sent down from time to time, to various peoples, through his many apostles and prophets. These books demonstrate God's greatest favour to mankind, for they are His means of guidance. The total number of books is believed, from the traditions, to be one hundred and four. Of these, only five are mentioned in the Qur'an:

- The *Scrolls of Abraham*, now lost;
- The *Taurat*, the books 'given' to Moses (which we know as the Pentateuch);
- The *Zabur*, or the Psalms 'given' to the prophet David;
- The *Injil*, or the gospel, 'given' to Jesus;
- The *Qur'an*, 'given' to the Last Prophet, Mohammed.

Some Muslims suggest that all other books, apart from the Qur'an, have been changed, altered and corrupted, in both language and content.

It is believed that the Qur'an in the Arabic language, as revealed to Mohammed, is an exact copy of the book which exists written on a special tablet in heaven. It was brought down to Mohammed by the angel Gabriel, who instructed Mohammed to recite it. As Arabic is the language of heaven any translation is reckoned to be an interpretation: the true Qur'an is considered untranslatable. Therefore when the Qur'an is so translated (or 'interpreted') Muslims will refrain from calling it by that name, using instead some suitable title that will describe it as 'an interpretation of the Holy Qur'an'.

iv. *Belief in the Prophets*: Two types of prophet are recognised in Islam: (a) the *nabi*: which includes anyone directly inspired by God. It is only a very general term. The Lord Jesus Christ is recognised as a great nabi, though, sadly, Muslims do not believe Him to have been more than this. It is interesting to note that He is also included in the other category of prophet, known as (b) *rasul*. These are distinguished prophets to whom a special message has been entrusted. There were, according to tradition, one hundred and twenty-four thousand *nabi*, but only three hundred and thirteen of these are to be identified as *rasul*. These are again subdivided, to include a group of nine *Ulu al 'Azam'*, 'possessors of power', namely, Noah, Abraham, David, Jacob, Joseph, Job, Moses, Jesus and Mohammed. Among these, six are granted special titles, for example, Abraham the Friend of God, Moses the Converser with God, Adam the Chosen of God, Jesus the Spirit of God. Beside these, and outside these groups, there are three recognised prophetesses: Sarah, who received the news of Isaac's birth by revelation; the mother of Moses, who similarly received the news of Moses' birth, and Mary, who received the news of Jesus the Messiah from an angel.

v. *Belief in the Day of Judgement*: This is a vital article of faith in Islam: that there is life after death in a wonderful Paradise. It is considered that

> "Our life on earth is temporary and is meant to be a preparation for *Akhirah* (life after death) which is never ending.

Life on this earth becomes meaningless if good actions are
not rewarded and bad conduct punished."

(Sarwar 1984:88)

One Muslim writer, Abuk A'la Mawdudi, lists the essential
ingredients of this belief:

a. There will be a Last Day, when life on earth will end
and everything will be annihilated.
b. God will sit in judgement on that day. All human
beings who have ever lived will be presented to Him.
c. The full record of everyone's good or bad deeds will be
presented to God.
d. Each person will be either rewarded if his good deeds
outweigh his bad ones, or punished if his bad outweigh his
good.
e. Those who are rewarded will go to Paradise; those who
are punished will go to hell.

(as listed in Cooper 1985: 42)

There are many graphic and highly colourful details ascribed
to the Last Day. The righteous will be given his book of deeds in
his right hand, but the damned will be forced to receive his in his
left hand. His works having been weighed in the balances,
everyone must walk the *syrat*, a path on the very brink of hell.
Great care has to be taken, for this path is described as a tight-rope
over the great chasm, a path sharper than a sword's edge, finer
than a hair. The righteous with his book in his right hand will walk
across into heaven, but the damned sinner will fall into the fires
of hell.

Heaven is a sensuous place, where men's desires are satis-
fied: a place of wonderful security and beautiful gardens, con-
taining vineyards full of ripe grapes; a place of shades and
fountains, with such an abundance of fruit as the heart may desire,
not to speak of the beautiful maidens who delight a man's heart!
There are said to be seven divisions in heaven, the highest being

called Paradise: and God's throne is above them all. There is no concept of the saved believer sharing in the glorified life and worship of God.

Hell, the other extreme, is spoken of with great respect and fear. The Qur'an makes frequent mention of the fires of hell, and popular books wax eloquent on the awful torments of the doomed. There is much confused thinking in evidence here, for although it is said that the righteous will pass over the hair's breadth bridge into heaven, orthodox teaching also states that all Muslims will spend time in hell, in a type of purgatory meant for their purification, but which therefore will not be everlasting. There are seven divisions of hell described: (i) *Jahannam*, the Muslim's purgatory; (ii) *Laza*, the fire dedicated to Christians(!); (iii) *Al Hutama*, the place designated for Jews; (iv) *Sa'ir*, the habitation of the Sabeans; (v) *Saqar*, set aside for the Magi; (vi) *Al-Jahim*, the huge fire reserved for idolators; and (vii) *Hawia*, the bottom pit appointed for hypocrites. The time one spends in hell depends on the severity of one's evil deeds, though there is some distinct feeling that levels (vi) and (vii) will remain for ever. It is a matter of some quite considerable debate!

The Signs of the Judgement Day are also elaborate, and of some interest to us:

a. The appearance of a mighty conqueror who will unite Muslims to become a great nation;

b. *Al Dajjal* (the Antichrist) will appear from between Iraq and Syria, roaming the world for forty days, laying it waste, before he is slain by the prophet Jesus;

c. Jesus Himself will return, take a wife, and have children. He will call everyone to accept Islam. During His forty years on earth, there will be peace as never known before, such as described in Isaiah 11:6. Then He will die, and be buried alongside Mohammed;

d. The sun will rise from the west;

e. The *Ka'aba* (the shrine of the stone in Mecca) will be destroyed. At the same time written copies of the Qur'an will be removed, and its words erased from people's memories;

f. This will be preceded by three blasts of a trumpet. The consequencies of this will be: that at the *first blast* all creatures in heaven and on earth will be struck with terror; at the *second blast* all creatures in heaven and on earth will die; and at the *third blast*, forty years later, all will be raised again for judgement.

This Day of Judgement will last one thousand years, or, maybe, even fifty thousand years (depending on which tradition!). When all are assembled for judgement the angels will keep them waiting for forty years (or another fifty thousand?). Then God Himself will appear. At that time Mohammed will intercede for all Muslims, because Adam, Noah, Abraham, Moses and Jesus will all decline to do so, feeling themselves to be unworthy of so great a task.

vi. *Belief in Predestination*: God is absolute in His decree of both good and evil. He alone gives life and causes death. His decrees are inescapable, and everything that happens is determined by Him and ordered in accordance with His absolute foreknowledge. These decrees are believed to be recorded by God's pen of fate on a preserved tablet. A Muslim believes that God is not limited by any consideration whatsoever, moral or otherwise. The matter alone rests with God as to whether He forgives or damns. God is the sole 'decider' of a man's deeds and destiny. This doctrine places the responsibility of all that a man does, whether good or evil, entirely upon God. Man is therefore deemed not responsible for what he does. On the other hand God cannot be accused of being unjust in judging those actions for which man cannot be held accountable. This precept is totally cold and clinical and has to be accepted blindly. Despite this somewhat irrational and harsh dogma, it is interesting to observe that in the hearts of many Muslims there is a deep-seated hunger and desire to know God. Consequently the practice of a great number of Muslims will be found to be inconsistent with this particular article of faith, though they will tenaciously hold to both a mental and verbal assent to it.

****

These are the six articles of faith that hold the Muslim brotherhood together. They are the common ground of the community of faith. The 'Pillars of Islam' are merely the tangible expression of these doctrines. We have not been able to look too closely at all the teaching of Islam. Many more areas of significance might profitably be looked at, in order to gain more insight into the Muslim community. The bibliography will indicate useful books that will help to give a broader and deeper understanding.

Part I

Conclusion

In this first section we have looked at the general situation with respect to Muslim beliefs and practices. If it has given the reader an appetite to know more, then it has fulfilled its intention. We live at a time when it is vital that Christians look more closely into this subject, because we are all coming into contact with Muslims to a far greater extent in our communities, and more opportunities are being given us to share our lives with them. We ought to have a desire to understand them with the following purpose in mind: that we may seek intelligently to lead them into an understanding of our own faith and of God's way of salvation. Let us not feel that we are being presumptuous in this task, for our Scriptures categorically state, and we are convinced of their truthfulness, that Jesus is the true revelation of God, and the only Saviour.

> **"Nor is there salvation in any other, for there is no other name given among men by which we must be saved".** (Acts 4:12)

We need to be aware that not many Muslims know the real doctrines of Islam which to them is very much a ritual. As long as they are seen to be doing the right things, and are thereby acceptable to, and accepted by, the Muslim community, all will be well. Islam is very plainly a system that proclaims salvation through works, and this is actually the reason why there is much ignorance on the finer points of doctrine. As those who seek to

present Christ to Muslims we need to know what they theoretically believe, but we must take care not to assume that the
individual Muslim actually knows what we assume he ought to
know! Let us not fall into the trap of teaching him his own
religion, when we are conversing with a Muslim in order to
present Christ to him. It may prove to be an easier task than we
think, especially if we are both considerate to him, and pray that
the Lord will prepare his heart to hear God's word.

It is the purpose of Part Two to help us consider how we may
bring Christ to the Muslim so that he may be saved through faith
in Christ. It has been the purpose of Part One to give us a
foundation on which to build our understanding of the one with
whom we are desiring to share Christ. May the Lord give us
wisdom to meet the need that we face: may He save to the
uttermost as He has promised.

PART TWO

PRESENTING THE WORD

Part II.

Introduction

The first question we need to ask ourselves when beginning to consider the challenge of Islam to the Christian faith, is: "How are we to present the gospel of grace to the Muslim?" We want him to come to know the Lord Jesus Christ, the Son of God, the express image of the Father, who upholds all things by the word of His power. We want to present *Him* who has purged us of our sins, who was raised from the dead to sit at the right hand of the Majesty on high, and who is the head of the Church, the true people of God, whom He has called by His sovereign grace.

How do we do what so often appears impossible to us? Our primary concern must be to get our own foundation right. We need to look for a valid *biblical approach* to the Muslim. We need to *use* the word of God. Many of us are familiar with doctrinal statements that may be similar to the following:

> "the Bible is the authoritative Word of God to all people, and a sure and complete guide in all matters of Christian thinking, living and service."   (We Believe 1983: 16)

This ought not to be merely theoretical. *The word of God is where we need to go* to understand our responsibility to the Muslim. To this end let us, in these next chapters, consider how our Scriptures relate to the problem that faces us. Not everyone may agree with the approach as presented. However, I appeal to you not to be put off, but rather to look at this very great problem in the light of the Scriptures and with an open mind and heart, determining, to the best of your ability, to understand how the

Lord would have Muslims saved by His grace.

As we come to consider how Christians are to view Islam and to approach Muslims with the gospel we have to start by making it clear that we do not accept the conclusions that Muslims arrive at with their particular world view. On our part, we believe that Islam is a false religion. This is of necessity, for the Lord Jesus Christ is the ultimate revelation of God to us. As Jesus Himself said,

> **"I and My Father are one."** John 10:30

> **"I am the way, the truth, and the life. No one comes to the Father except through Me."** John 14:6

> **"Do you not believe that I am in the Father, and the Father in Me? The words that I speak to you I do not speak on My own authority; but the Father who dwells in Me does the works. Believe Me that I am in the Father and the Father in Me, or else believe Me for the sake of the works themselves."** John 14:10-11

The apostle Peter adds his own succinct commentary to this truth:

> **"Nor is there salvation in any other, for there is no other name under heaven given among men by which we must be saved."** Acts 4:12

If any other name is put forward and claimed to bring a revelation of God to the world, especially one that comes after Christ, we are to understand it to be '*antichrist*'. We have our witness to this in the Scriptures:

> **"Who is a liar but he who denies that Jesus is the Christ? He is antichrist who denies the Father and the Son."** 1 John 2:22

"...every spirit that does not confess that Jesus Christ has come in the flesh is not of God. And this is the spirit of the antichrist . . ."   1 John 4:3

"For many deceivers have gone out into the world who do not confess Jesus Christ as coming in the flesh. This is a deceiver and an antichrist."   2 John 7

This conclusion of the Apostle John is well supported by our Lord's own words, for He gives His own warning:

"...many false prophets will rise up and deceive many. .. Then if anyone says to you, 'Look, here is the Christ!' or 'There!' do not believe it. For false christs and false prophets will arise and show great signs and wonders, so as to deceive, if possible, even the elect."
                                                    Matthew 24:11, 23-24

Islam must therefore be, on a biblical understanding, a deception from Satan. You may have thought Part I of this treatise was perhaps a little pro-Islam; that it wasn't critical enough! This was deliberate. I had in mind that there is so much anti-Islamic thinking among western Christians, not born of informed criticism, but which originates from prejudice. This has resulted in a situation where we not only rightly hate Islam as a satanic deception, but we come to hate the people too. We need to learn to love the people: to love Muslims who are in subjection to the Islamic way of thinking. All too often we have thought of Muslims in a negative manner. We must learn to consider them in a positive way. We must learn to understand where they are (the purpose of Part I), in order to take them on to something far greater: to know the saving grace of God. In this way we may bring down the strongholds of Satan, and we can do it with the word of God. I trust that Part II goes some way toward giving direction to our thinking and practice in this respect.

6.
A Biblical Background to Islam

Islam appears to be a post-Christian phenomenon. Historically this cannot be doubted, arising as it did in the 7th century A.D. Can Islam be appropriately and properly addressed by our Christian Scriptures? Surely the Bible does not speak to the subject of Islam? These questions may appear on the surface to be disturbing, daunting, and even disconcerting. Let us face up to this challenge, and seek to discover whether we can after all find appropriate answers in the Scriptures.

The Bible does *not* address itself specifically to the problem of Islam. Even though Muslims claim that they see references that anticipate the coming of Mohammed (e.g. John 14:16!), there is no place in the Bible that prophetically speaks of the teaching of Islam. Yet we positively and confidently state that we believe there is nothing outside the scope of the word of God; not even Islam. The message of the Bible is always that human nature, aspirations and ideas do not radically change, but only in their outward appearance. The principles taught by Islam, therefore, were not new in themselves; not even in Mohammed's day.

We stated in our introduction to this section that Islam is satanic in its origins. Yet Satan knows what he is doing to a limited degree; he knows how to confuse the issues. His strategy is to mix truth with error so craftily that the confusion is not readily discerned. Therefore, we can state that some of the ideas he presents do have a basis of truth. It is this subtlety that makes Islam appear surprisingly attractive and consequently so difficult to deal with.

A close look at Islam reveals that it has a pre-Christian

philosophy and ethos. A great deal of the Qur'an embodies Old
Testament thought and history, though some of the allusions
must be recognised as factually incorrect.

Islam is a system that is based on law. It holds to a doctrine
of works which includes worship and sacrifice akin to what we
observe in the Old Testament. There were identifiable periods in
Mohammed's life in which he was deeply interested in Jewish
teaching. Therefore, as we note the ingredients that make up the
basic principles of Islam, we begin to see the possibility of
drawing distinct parallels.

A biblical understanding begins to dawn when we note that
the Muslim faith originated among Arabs who claimed to be
descendants of Ishmael. In our usual reading of the book of
Genesis we rather tend to overlook Ishmael. We discount him
and concern ourselves with Isaac, the son of promise. However,
the story of Ishmael is relevant to our understanding of the
Muslim. We observe that God made some very specific promises
with respect to Ishmael. First, to his mother, Hagar:

> **"The angel of the Lord said, 'I will multiply your de-
> scendants exceedingly, so that they shall not be
> counted for multitude... Behold you are with child,
> and you shall bear a son. You shall call his name
> Ishmael (meaning 'God hears'), because the Lord has
> heard your affliction. He shall be a wild man; his hand
> shall be against every man, and every man's hand
> against him.'"**   Genesis 16:10-12 *

There is no doubt that Abraham loved his son Ishmael very
deeply. We find him pleading on Ishmael's behalf with God:

---

* *Other promises to note: Genesis 21:8-21. References of
interest with respect to Ishmael include Genesis 25:9,13-17;
28:9; 36:3,10.*

> **"Oh, that Ishmael might live before You!"**
> Genesis 17:18

God responded by giving Abraham this promise of His mercy and grace:

> **". . . as for Ishmael, I have heard you. Behold, I have blessed him, and will make him fruitful, and will multiply him exceedingly. He shall beget twelve princes, and I will make him a great nation."**
> Genesis 17:20

Perhaps we should not be quite so surprised at the great wealth and diplomatic power that Middle Eastern Muslims (Arabs) appear to display today. Islam is, sadly, the spiritual heritage of Ishmael, Abraham's son of a bondwoman.

In addition, we do need to face Islam from a New Testament perspective, and it will be helpful to use some relevant guidelines from the Gospels and the Epistles. We have established that Islam is a system of law demanding an absolute and unquestioning obedience in order to gain merit and approval with God. It is encouraging to note that our Lord Jesus Christ faced this very same challenge in the Pharisees. Indeed, the Lord personally described them to us in the following manner:

> **"The scribes and the Pharisees sit in Moses' seat. . . They bind heavy burdens, hard to bear, and lay them on men's shoulders . . . all their works they do to be seen of men."**
> Matthew 23:2,4,5

He also portrays their self-righteousness in these very descriptive terms:

> ". . . they say, and do not do . . . blind guides .
> . . hypocrites! . . . Woe to you, for you cleanse
> the outside of the cup and dish, but inside they
> are full of extortion and self-indulgence . . .
> whitewashed tombs which indeed appear beau-
> tiful outwardly, but inside are full of dead men's
> bones and all uncleanness."
>
> Matthew 23:3,16,23,25,27

The Lord adds an observation which is also very pertinent and
in keeping with Muslim practices. He relates that they

> "build the tombs of the prophets and adorn the
> monuments of the righteous."   Matthew 23:29

Our Lord gives us a very vivid description of the Muslim
through the portrait of the Pharisee in one of His parables:

> "He spoke this parable to some who trusted in
> themselves that they were righteous, and de-
> spised others... The Pharisee stood and prayed
> thus with himself, 'God, I thank You that I am
> not like other men — extortioners, unjust, adul-
> terers, or even as this tax-collector. I fast twice
> a week; I give tithes of all that I possess.'"
>
> Luke 18:11-12

We learn a great deal by considering carefully how the Lord
dealt with the Pharisees. Did He not present the gospel of grace
to one known as Nicodemus? This also is worthy of our
discerning examination, attention and thoughtful study.

7.
A Biblical Approach to Islam

Several details with respect to a Christian's attitude and position ought to be considered. We may understand much that Islam teaches, but we must also ensure that our own approach is not hindering our genuine desire to draw Muslims to the foot of the cross. Let us therefore prayerfully consider the following points.

i. *We need to recognise that we cannot reach Muslims in our own strength.*

It is the Holy Spirit who applies the truth of God's word. We face a powerful spiritual battle in Islam. Muslims are in the stronghold of Satan. A real spiritual oppression can be experienced in Muslim countries. This knowledge surely requires us to take careful stock of the situation. It necessitates that we make certain we are well-equipped with the spiritual armour made available to us (Ephesians 6:10-18). It demands that we be resolute and watchful in prayer. It ought to compel us to pray that the Holy Spirit will open blind eyes and overcome the problems of misunderstanding — that is, for us, as well as for the Muslim. We must pray that, by His sovereign power, the Lord may call those who are to come to a saving knowledge of Christ. I believe there are two fundamental factors that are required of us, namely, (i) to believe that God will fulfil the promises of His word as we seek to serve Him faithfully; and (ii) to experience the anointing and filling of the Holy Spirit so that we will be enabled to withstand the onslaught and counter-attack of Satan. Let us not underestimate his ability to retaliate.

ii. *We need to be totally committed to God and conscientiously obedient to the two great commandments.*

> **"You shall love the Lord your God with all your heart, with all your soul, and with all your mind, and with all your strength... You shall love your neighbour as yourself."**   Mark 12:30,31

Without such a life of dedication and close fellowship with the Lord, no one will win through the strongholds of Satan. Without this relationship with God all attempts to witness to the Muslim will fail. We must learn what it means to love our Muslim neighbour as ourselves. These are fundamentals that must be heeded.

Such a life of total commitment and a meaningful love for the Lord speaks volumes to the Muslim observer. We need to approach Muslims with a spirit of humility, to seek to establish a rapport and basis of trust with them. It would be very rash indeed to come alongside Muslims with an attitude that plainly tells them that we think they are completely wrong, but that we, of course, have it all right! We will have lost both the attention and respect of our Muslim friends. They simply will not listen to us. Preferably, let us conform as far as possible to the example of the apostle Paul:

> **"though I am free from all men, I have made myself a servant to all, that I might win the more; ... to the Jews I became as a Jew, that I might win Jews; to those who are under the law, as under the law, that I might win those who are under the law ... I have become all things to all men, that I might by all means save some. .. this I do for the gospel's sake."** 1 Corinthians 9:19-23

For the sake of clarity of exposition we must take into account Paul's use of the word "*as*" in this passage. We are not expected to compromise our position as Christians in order to take on a

Muslim identity. That is not what Paul is teaching here. We are not to put ourselves under bondage because of those whom we are trying to reach. We are, nevertheless, to do all we can to get alongside the Muslim so that we may present the message of the grace of God to him in terms he can understand. We are to place ourselves willingly in a position where we may deny ourselves things that we would normally accept in our own sphere of life and work; we are to be happy to place on one side those things that may offend our Muslim friend, in our desire to understand and approach him. We must personally be constantly seeking not to be an offence to him. There is enough offence in the gospel itself, without *our* being the offence. For this reason, it is wise for us to consider that we may need to adapt our ways, our pattern of life, and our thinking, to bring them more into line with those whom we desire to lead to Christ.

iii. *We need to use language appropriately.*

In Acts 21:37-40 we find that Paul changed the language he used so as to speak appropriately to different groups of people. He recognised the importance of distinguishing the personal and cultural language (sometimes called 'heart language'), from the 'trade language' of the people with whom he was conversing. Paul was seeking to obtain a direct and personal response. We must also recognise that, even if we use English, our native tongue, we must use a vocabulary that is both understandable and pertinent to the Muslim. We want to use all means to avoid being misunderstood, and to prevent the wrong implication being made from what we say. We will want to take all precautions against giving the wrong impressions when we are speaking to Muslims about eternal issues. I believe that it is a biblical principle to start where the people are, even if their understanding of a particular word or idea is inadequate or incomplete, and to bring our own teaching to bear at the appropriate time. It is our indisputable intention to build a correct understanding and knowledge of the truth of God. We must be very sensitive to the Muslims' weaknesses in this area. We must seek to lead them on lovingly

and carefully in their understanding so that they may come to
appreciate concepts that they have never known before.

iv. *We need to have a biblical attitude to culture.*

Muslim culture reflects the way a Muslim thinks and what he
believes. For this reason some Christians have not found any
aspect of Muslim culture acceptable, having interpreted it only in
the light of Muslim ideology. Certainly, cultural values are
strongly influenced by the religious beliefs of a people, but we
surely cannot reject their whole culture out of hand without
rejecting the people themselves. The apostle Peter learnt something of this lesson, I suggest, when he saw a vision of a great
sheet in which there were all kinds of livestock.

> **"And a voice came to him, 'Rise, Peter; kill and eat.'
> But Peter said, 'Not so Lord! For I have never eaten
> anything common or unclean.' And a voice spoke to
> him again . . . 'What God has cleansed [declared
> clean] you must not call common.'"**
>
> Acts 10:12-15

In this case Peter had to see his own cultural inhibitions in
their true light. He experienced many restraints because of Old
Testament rituals and laws that were centred on the Old Covenant. Christ had now fulfilled all the legal requirements of the
Old Covenant, but Peter found difficulty in applying this truth in
the light of some preconceived notions that his society accepted.
One of his problems was a prejudice against the Gentiles. They
were not included under the covenant, but rather positively
excluded, and the general conclusion was that the people of God
should have nothing to do with them. Yet it was in the Lord's
purposes that the Gentiles should be blessed through the privileges that were experienced by the Jews. Had not God made this
promise to the Old Testament people of God?

> **"The Gentiles shall come to your light, and kings to the**

> **brightness of your rising ... The wealth of the Gentiles shall come to you ... To the name of the Lord your God, and to the Holy One of Israel, because He has glorified you."**   Isaiah 60:3,5,9

God promised through the prophets that He would send his Servant, the Messiah, one to be born a Son, who would be the means of bringing this to reality. Thus God assures his Servant:

> **"It is too small a thing that You should be My Servant. ..to restore the preserved ones of Israel; I will also give You as a light to the Gentiles, that You should be my salvation to the ends of the earth."**   Isaiah 49:6

Therefore the gospel must be seen to cross the limitations of cultural as well as religious boundaries. Through Christ, men and women from all cultural backgrounds are to be called into God's Kingdom.

Peter overcame his prejudice against the Gentiles. We too must recognise that all of us have natural, or should I say, culturally conditioned prejudices against, and negative responses to, any pattern of life that differs from our own. We must therefore heed the Lord's calling and respond as Peter did. We must come to accept Muslims where they are, and as they are; we must accept them, their way of thinking and cultural practices, for that is where they are at the moment. It is only as we learn to accept Muslims as people that they will begin to listen to us and want to try to understand what we are saying to them. We must first learn to befriend Muslims before we can hope to win confidences on which to base a pertinent presentation of the gospel of grace.

It must be stated that the application of the gospel itself will bring about significant cultural changes. In particular those elements that are positively sinful within any cultural setting will be dealt with. We must allow the gospel message to do its own work by applying biblical truth in appropriate and sensitive ways.

In other words we must take care not to attempt to do the gospel's work in our own strength and wisdom. The gospel will also remould those things which are indifferent, subjecting everything to its influence. In this way, through the work of the Holy Spirit in convicting sin and teaching the truth by applying the word of God, culture will necessarily bow to the authority of the Son of God, the Lord of glory. The application of the gospel message will also infuse those things that are specifically significant for the Christian walk and way of life. It is the gospel that will change culture; such change is not our direct responsibility. We find some very clear principles in Romans 14 that we must take into account. Paul could clearly and positively state:

> **"I know and am convinced by the Lord Jesus that there is nothing unclean of itself... Yet if your brother is grieved because of your food, you are no longer walking in love. Do not destroy with your food the one for whom Christ died."** Romans 14:14,15

Though the Apostle is speaking of a Christian brother in particular, the principle must surely also hold true for one whom we are seeking to win for Christ. Paul continues:

> **"Do not destroy the work of God for the sake of food. All things indeed are pure, but it is evil for the man who eats with offence."** Romans 14:20

We must take care not to give offence. The Muslim, for example, is offended by the Christian eating pork. We must admit that in reality we can take pork, or leave it: it is not an issue to us. Yet so often when we face this problem we defend ourselves, and claim that it is our right to eat pork: that no-one is going to take that 'right' away from us for any reason — "I am going to eat pork, regardless of what you say!" Should we do that when we are trying to win this Muslim brother? Let us take care not to get high-minded and arrogant, asserting that we are free in this area: that Christ brings freedom for us here. He does. But He also gives us freedom to say, "No" to the things that are indifferent to us. It is right to consider that we may have to adapt our ways, our pattern of life, our thinking, so that we may not cause offence to those with whom we are sharing the gospel. We will want to bring all we do into line with those whom we desire to lead to Christ, as far as it is possible and legitimate to so, so that we achieve our stated aim **"that I might by all means save some."** Our liberty includes the freedom to abstain from anything that may cause offence, for the sake of the gospel.

> **"It is good neither to eat meat nor drink wine nor do anything by which your brother stumbles or is offended or is made weak."** Romans 14:21

v. *We need to understand the Muslim thought patterns.*

It must also be reasonable to consider that we shall need to understand the direction of Muslim thought. *How* do Muslims think, and *why* do they think in the particular way that they do? How does their thought pattern consequently affect their lives? This is necessary to know so that we may proclaim the gospel message in terms that they will understand and find acceptable. It is our longing to be able to present the gospel, the truth of God, in a meaningful and purposeful way to the Muslim. This is not to suggest that we must compromise truth in any way whatsoever. We do not change the gospel, or any of its message, to reach the Muslim. But we may present it in terms that they find reasonable and acceptable. We may take the biblical example of Paul on Mars Hill. There in Athens he had noticed an altar inscribed *"To the unknown God"*. Paul used this as a point of contact and spoke to the philosophers of Athens about the living God whom they did not know but who had revealed Himself in Christ. Paul also appealed to one of their own authors to make a theological truth appropriately meaningful:

> "for in Him we live and move and have our being, as also some of your own poets have said, 'For we are also His offspring.' Therefore, since we are the offspring of God, we ought not to think that the Divine Nature is like gold or silver or stone, something shaped by art and man's devising."   Acts 17:28-29

Paul takes his hearers from where they are in their understanding, and leads them unoffensively to where they need to be for a right and true appreciation of the gospel. We need to start, therefore, with the Muslim's own comprehension of the nature of God. We may build on it (and seek gradually to cut away by a positive affirmation of truth those ideas that are in error) and take him on further to know the clear revelation of God in Christ. To attempt to destroy the Muslim perception, as inadequate as it is, will cause him to shut his ears to the gospel, for he may very well read into our rejection of his beliefs a rejection of himself. How much we need to pray that the Holy Spirit will set forth the glories of Christ and apply His saving grace to the Muslim heart. We also need to pray that the Holy Spirit may over-rule all the inadequacies of *our presentation* of the glorious gospel of sovereign grace.

8.
Facing Muslim Misunderstandings

We come now to consider what the Muslim thinks we believe. Various doctrines of the Christian faith have become great problems to the Muslim mind. He misunderstands much of what we believe to be the fundamentals of Christian doctrine. It is easy to dismiss this aspect of our discussion as unimportant. But we must face up to the fact that the opposite is true. We cannot assume that when we use a certain term to describe an aspect of truth the Muslim will understand it in the way that we intend (see Appendix 3). We must do all we can to safeguard against all wrong interpretations. We must avoid using terms which will communicate somthing other than what we are trying to say. Therefore, we must ask, what is the Muslim concept of Christian dogma? What does he *think* we believe?

1. The Trinity
This is a paramount stumbling-block. 'God is One', asserts the Muslim. None can be associated with Him, and He certainly cannot have a Son. The Muslim also adds, "He is 'totally other'", that is, so very different from anything man can imagine. Therefore no-one can describe God to us, nor can anyone show us what He is like.

Mohammed had only spoken with heretical Christians, and he was totally misled. Consequently these wrong ideas have been perpetuated down through the centuries. Muslims are taught from a very young age that Christians believe in three gods: the Father, Mary the Mother, and the Son. The Sonship of Jesus is only understood in terms of gross materialism: that Jesus was the offspring of Mary through a purely physical relationship, God having assumed the form of a man for this to take place. Mohammed would have been aware of the Nestorian-Monophysite controversy, originating in the 5th century, over the term "Mother of God" as applied to Mary, and it certainly would not have helped the situation. That term had become widely used, instead of "Mother of Christ". There is consequently a positive assertion to be found in the Qur'an concerning this heresy:

> "Unbelievers are those that say: 'Allah is one of three.' There is but one God..... Allah will say: 'Jesus, son of Mary, did you ever say to mankind: "Worship me and my mother as gods beside Allah"?.'"
>
> (Qur'an: Sura 5: 73, 116)

Jesus is said by the Qur'an to have denied this indignity. The orthodox Christian must also agree, for the concept of three gods is just as offensive in Christianity as it is in Islam. We believe in one God, who reveals *Himself* in Trinity (three Persons). Interestingly, the Qur'an maintains a virgin birth of Jesus through the mediation of the Holy Spirit almost in opposition to this terrible misunderstanding and blasphemous idea.

2. The Person of Jesus

Jesus the Messiah is greatly respected as the penultimate Prophet, but Muslims despise the cult of Christianity, as they see it, that has arisen around Him. Muslims usually deny His crucifixion and consequent resurrection, though the Qur'anic verse on which they base this is an ambiguous one, allowing various possible interpretations. It is common to argue that another person took His place on the cross (for it is not denied that there was a crucifixion), Jesus Himself being taken directly into heaven. The Qur'an contains many traditional beliefs about Jesus, but we must never assume that the Muslim is rejecting the Jesus of our faith: he is not. He does not know Him. As Bishop Stephen Neill states:

"It is not the case that the Muslim has seen Jesus of
Nazareth and rejected him; he has never seen him, and the
veil of misunderstanding and prejudice is still over his
face."   (quoted in Goldsmith 1982: 60)

It is important to understand that Muslims have never in fact
rejected the gospel as we perceive it. Their apparent resistance
is related to the fact that they have not understood its message.

3. The Scriptures

In the Muslim view of revelation the word of God is first
written in heaven. God gives His word to men, the final and
complete revelation being the Qur'an, transmitted by the archan-
gel Gabriel. The Qur'an is believed to be a perfect replica of the
eternal word. Its perfection lies in the idea that there was no
human interference in its transmission. It is maintained that
Mohammed only received it by dictation. This assertion has
resulted in two emphases: (i) that Mohammed is projected as
having been illiterate and therefore incapable of personal involvement in forming the text; (ii) that any translation of the
Qur'an from the Arabic is impossible, for it thus becomes an
interpretation and no longer a replica of God's word.

Another problem lies in what a Muslim perceives of the *Injil*,
our Gospels. We are used to the fact that they have been written
by the evangelists, namely, Matthew, Mark, Luke and John.
Their description is therefore "*The Gospel according to Matthew*, etc." Yet the Muslim looks for the actual Gospel that was
with God in heaven which was revealed through Jesus. He does
not want Matthew's version, or any man's account of Jesus. The
Muslim therefore deduces that the Christians have lost the
original Gospel, and that they have corrupted the Scriptures to
their own ends. Muslims find it difficult to accept the Gospels as
they are, and thus the gospel message, because they believe that
we do not have the original word of God.

The problem is further enhanced when the Muslim picks up
and examines a reference Bible and sees *alternative readings*

given. The Muslim is looking for the actual words which God revealed, but the Christian is unable to produce what he demands. The problem is compounded by the factor of so many Bible versions today. There is no authoritative text. Furthermore, there are the contradictions between the Qur'an and the New Testament. We end up with a very bewildered Muslim, and we have to face what seems almost an insurmountable difficulty.

Notwithstanding, we have the conviction that our Scriptures are the full revelation of God. We confidently assert that they do not merely contain the word of God, but that they are God's authoritative word. Therefore they are not to be argued about, but used! The Scriptures have been given by the sovereign power of the Holy Spirit working in the hearts of godly men. The writing of the books of Scripture has been governed by the Holy Spirit; they are applied by the Holy Spirit, and prove to be **"sharper than any two-edged sword."** We must recognise the ultimate truth that we, personally, are weak, but that the Holy Spirit and His word are strong, and that, as our Lord Jesus Christ, the living Word, asserted,

> **"without Me you can do nothing."**   John 15: 5

The Scriptures themselves witness to the truth that all things are possible to him who believes. The Lord has already demonstrated that He is able to bring Muslims to a saving knowledge of Christ despite the difficulties that we see. The glory will never be ours: it must always, must necessarily be, His!

4. The Word of God

We interpret the 'word of God' to mean the revelation of and true knowledge of God, which carries His complete authority. So does the Muslim. He contends that the Qur'an fits that description, for it is uncreated and eternally with God in heaven. Interestingly this title, Word of God, is often applied to Jesus the Messiah in the Qur'an. As Christians we recognise Jesus as the Word of God, as having existed from eternity, as uncreated: the eternal Word. He, in Himself, is the complete, authoritative revelation of God to man. Muslims believe that the complete will of God is revealed in the Qur'an; that the Qur'an is therefore the living word of God, a miracle in itself. Christians hold that Jesus is the living Word of God, the incarnate Word. The Christian also asserts that the Holy Bible is God's word, in the sense that it is God's revealed will and purpose for mankind; that it is the written account of the life and ministry of Jesus, revealing Him fully and that it is given by inspiration of God (2 Timothy 3:15-17; 2 Peter 1:19-21). The Scriptures, as the written word of God, reveal His will for man as demonstrated in the perfect life of Jesus Christ. The focal point of the Scriptures is the Lord Jesus Christ: they all centre on Him and find their fulfilment in Him. Jesus in Himself is the complete revelation of God Himself to all mankind. He is:

> **"the brightness of His glory and the express image of His person."**
>   Hebrews 1:3

If we are to compare Christian faith and Islam beliefs, we must take care how we do so. We need to ask what the Qur'an really means to the Muslim:

> "It is essential to realise that the Qur'an is to the Muslim what Jesus is to the Christian. It is a mistake to make a direct comparison between the role of Jesus in Christianity and the role of Muhammad in Islam, or between the place of the Bible in Christianity and the place of the Qur'an in Islam."
>   (Chapman 1983: 31)

Mohammed's message to his people was the Qur'an, but the message of Christianity is the *person* of Christ. This is an important distinction which must not be misunderstood.

5. Faith

The Muslim identifies faith as identical with obedience and

conformity to God's revealed law. Therefore for the Muslim *works* are *synonymous with* faith. To quote a published Muslim sermon,

> "Faith is the devoting of the heart unto God by man and his acceptance of what God has revealed to His Prophets, his belief in His determination and His Will. It is a breath from the spirit of God, by which He confirms those who sincerely believe . . . It is a torch lighted from the light of God, irradiating into the hearts of the chosen ones among those who love Him. Faith has signs that point the way to it. . . These are the indications of the true faith: the fear of God which impels a man to magnify Him and extol Him, meditation on His signs which stimulates him to trust in His promise, reliance upon God leading him to conformity to His decree, so that he reverences Him in his prayers and is obedient in his almsgiving". quoted in Cragg 1956: 128

Acts of obedience are not merely the expression of faith. The Muslim mind conceives of the works themselves as faith. Muslim faith is not a total commitment to a person, as for the Christian to the Lord Jesus Christ, but commitment to a system of works. His faith is not expressed in love to God, but in doing what is expected of him, according to the rules laid down. As the Muslim sermon quotation above clearly points out, faith is based on the fear of the consequences of non-obedience. Faith, to the Muslim, is not thought of as appropriating the gift of salvation and mercy by a repentant sinner. The Muslim views faith as the means of earning salvation and the way to merit God's mercy. To use the word *faith* with respect to Islam is really to describe the universal oneness that is observed in the ritual of Islam, the conformity and uniformity displayed. It can only be understood as an unreasoned and mechanical observance of the laws of Islam.

Having made the very subtle distinctions above, one has to

admit that it is in fact difficult to hold them in balance on the practical level. Yet we must be careful when we use the term 'faith', or hear a Muslim use it, that we do not assume that we are talking about precisely the same concept.

6. Sin

Muslims stress that man was created good, but being made of clay he was inherently weak and fallible by nature. Thus sin in Muslim thought is merely making a mistake, a failure to conform to the will of God. There is no concept of original sin or of a transmissible corrupt nature. The Muslim is deeply aware of human weakness, but he will deny any inbuilt proneness to sin. He has a very superficial understanding of what sin is. Particular acts of sin become insignificant and of no consequence. The Muslim will focus on the penalty of sin, rather than admit responsibility for the 'mistake' that he makes. To be caught out and exposed in committing a 'wrong' act is a matter of shame and embarrassment, rather than of feeling and admitting guilt. To take the example of stealing, the sin is in being found out, rather than the act of taking what does not belong to you. This must be understood in terms of the absolute will of God which decrees how a man will act. (see Chapter 5: vi. Belief in Predestination, p. 48)

For the Christian the concept of sin is very substantial. It is essentially opposition, and disobedience, to the divine will. It can be defined in terms of lawlessness, rebellion, unrighteousness, missing the mark (God's standard); it is an affront to the holiness and righteousness of God. The attitude of sinfulness and the performance of sin carry with them the burden of personal responsibility. The sinner will have to answer to God for his attitudes and actions: he is totally responsible.

7. Salvation

This concept is only understood in terms of submission to God's will through obedience. One is 'saved' solely through doing good works, but it is even then entirely at the discretion of

God. It is conceived as obtaining admittance to a sensual Paradise. There is no assurance, no assured expectation or hope, of eternal life.

The Christian view of salvation is in terms of the recovery of what has been lost through sin. It is described as redemption, rescue, and being saved from the just consequences of sin. The Christian understands that a sinner is unable to help himself, but that God, by an act of kindness and mercy, is able to meet the righteous demands of His own holy will, and reach out to the sinner by grace. It is the perfect Son of God who alone was able to turn the wrath of God away from guilty sinners, by the perfect sacrifice of His own life. By grace, the sinner is enabled to believe savingly on the Lord Jesus Christ, to receive forgiveness of sin. He is made acceptable to God, not on his own merit, but solely on the basis of Christ's obedience to the Father's will. Salvation involves, for the Christian, the receiving of a new spiritual birth and the ability to live a life that is pleasing to God. Salvation comes to sinners through the dynamic love of God for sinners whom He determines to save.

8. Sanctification

Any concept of the holy life, and of being made holy, that the Muslim may hold, is in terms of obedience to the law. He looks for the merit that is to be gained by good works and by performing religious ritual. One must seek to gain the approval of God by all means available.

For the Christian, sanctification is the outworking of eternal life in the soul of the believer in the Lord Jesus Christ, by the gracious operations of the Holy Spirit. It is the practical application of the truth that the sinner has been renewed in the image of God. It is learning to live a life of obedience in love to the God who first loved us.

It is also understood, more specifically, that sanctification is obedience to the revealed moral law. The Ten Commandments are not abrogated by the grace and mercy of God in the Lord Jesus Christ, but become the standard of the Christian's life, and his aim is thus to be like Christ in His obedience to His Father's revealed will. Sanctification for the Christian is the process by which the believer aims and works, in co-operation with the Holy Spirit, for a perfect obedience to the revealed law and commandments of God, a perfection not reached in this life.

We must take great care to distinguish between the biblical concepts of sanctification and justification, in the light of Muslim thought. The Christian cannot become righteous in God's sight by any obedience to the law of God. Righteousness is entirely the gift of God to the sinner, appropriated by means of the faith that God himself gives, and is therefore understood to be entirely of the grace of God. He is assured of God's work of salvation in his own heart, that he has been made acceptable to God only through the merits of Christ's perfect obedience, having been cleansed by His shed blood, and thus covered by *His* righteousness. Having become a new creation in Christ the believer is then enabled by the power of God to begin to obey God's law and to live by it. Therefore the law does not, cannot, save us, but it is the standard by which we live as those who have come to know salvation (i.e. justification through faith alone) in the Lord Jesus Christ.

9. Love

There is no appreciation of God as the God of love, for Muslims believe that He is unknowable and remote. The Muslim view is that no-one may have any relationship with Him. To suggest such a relationship is akin to *associating with God* (which is the Muslim concept of *shirk*). Such an idea is both wrong and unforgivable.

The Christian view of love is the basis of the revelation of God Himself to man. He is love. It is His nature to love. This love is eternally shared and reciprocated by the three Persons of the Godhead. It is this same love that God desired to share with those whom He created. In sending Jesus Christ into the world, God was sharing His love with mankind. The whole of the life and ministry of Jesus Christ was motivated and evidenced by love. It is through salvation that sinners come to appreciate God's love, become sharers of His love, and are given the assurance that they will continue to do so for eternity.

N.B. We must take exceedingly great care that all the terms we may use with Muslims are carefully explained first. It is dangerous to assume that our Muslim friend understands them the same way as we do.

The above considerations, though neither detailed nor comprehensive, show us something of the magnitude of the challenge that we have in confronting the Muslim with the claims of Christ and His salvation. We need to pray for wisdom in each situation in which we have the opportunity to witness to Muslims. We must pray that our love both for the Lord and for the Muslim himself will win through. We are limited, but we have the encouragement that, in the face of the seemingly impossible, *the Lord has power to save.*

9.
Making Known The Gospel Message (1)

As we come now to our central concern, we need to consider how we may approach the Muslim with the gospel in a sensible and godly way.

1. Evaluate Our Attitude

Above all else we must *apply ourselves to prayer*. We have to recognise that we need to admit our own weakness and cry out to Him who is able to fulfil His purposes for us (Psalm 57:2). It is prayer that puts, and keeps us, in touch with the one who desires to draw all men to Himself. All our efforts will result in failure if we go forward in our own strength. We *need* the power of God. We must be aware that this is not only to give us confidence in the work in which we are involving ourselves. We also need to ask that the Holy Spirit will prepare the heart of the one to whom we may speak, whoever he may be. We must pray too that we shall receive wisdom and understanding. We need to know that the words we may employ will be those which the Holy Spirit directs us to use in those particular circumstances. God knows the heart of the Muslim, and his situation; we do not. We must necessarily know His guidance in our thoughts and in our speech.

Respect their beliefs: Paul set us a tremendous example as he created a relationship with the philosophers on Mars Hill. When he quoted from among their authors, among other things he disarmed their natural antagonism to him, and perhaps even to his message to a great extent, and by so doing established a basis of acceptance for his teaching on their part. It was a platform from which to launch into a clear exposition of the revealed biblical truth. The Apostle did not ridicule, or try to show up the false basis of their thinking: instead he built upon their inadequate understanding.

Consider their feelings: The tenets of Islam are the basis of the Muslim pattern of life. Everything that a Muslim does is dependent on them. These principles are dear to Muslims, and therefore any frontal attack on their beliefs will immediately cut off your avenue of communication. Better to show them love and genuine concern, with the desire that they might come to have a deeper and correct understanding of God and His will for them.

Understand their problems: We must realise that even though they may have many misconceptions about the Christian faith, Muslims have been taught them from childhood. These ideas are therefore ingrained into their thought-patterns. As a result their prejudices are very deep-seated. It is only as we appreciate that they can only change these perceptions at great cost to their personal feelings of security, and even personal integrity, that we may begin to appreciate in some measure the immensity of our task.

Be sensitive to the possibility of communicating the wrong thing: We must be willing, and take time, to explain all our terms, religious or otherwise, very carefully. In seeking to convey important concepts, be careful in the choice of the words you use and be careful to explain the meaning of terms that may be misunderstood. It is wise to consider using only those terms that will be helpful to the Muslim listener at whatever stage he has reached in his understanding.

Take only one step at a time: We are not required to present the whole case with respect to the gospel all at once. We need to present each aspect of truth clearly and meaningfully as far as our Muslim friend is able both to accept and understand it. We must take care not to be too impatient. We must not rush what we are doing. We have a glorious gospel and we want it to be seen in that light. We must not feel a failure if we are not able to present every aspect of the gospel at any one time: we are more likely to be a failure if we attempt to do so!

Encourage a basis of friendship and trust before overtly

sharing gospel truth. We should find that our Muslim friend will be able to accept what we are saying far more readily, if he feels that we are not too great a threat to him. He will be less on his guard, and more ready to listen to what we are actually saying.

Take care not to cause offence in anything, or in any way. This applies equally to what we may say, what we may wear, what we may eat; indeed, whatever we may do. Our relationship with God, our understanding of His word, our life of faith are all very special and meaningful to us. Therefore we must act accordingly: we must behave reverently and respectfully. We must never, in any circumstance, appear off-hand or casual in dealing with the things of God.

2. Consider Legitimate Points Of Contact

Our Muslim friend would be very happy for us to *pray with him*. Sadly this is often the last thing a Christian will think about in his relationship with a Muslim: it should be the first! It would be good for him to be able to see how natural our relationship is with God, and how important prayer is to us. It is extremely wise for us to make a note that he usually considers a Christian to be a person who does *not* pray!

He will appreciate not only the praise of God and the giving of thanks for His many blessings, but also praying particularly for him and his family. We can pray that they may be blessed of God, that they may receive His mercy, and His healing power (in the case of ill-health). Appropriate and applied prayer will speak volumes to a Muslim. It is also fitting to remember in prayer that God knows us and our weaknesses, and that we are all like sheep having gone astray. We may include all these concepts, and we can pray in the name of Jesus as we ought to.

Posture in prayer could well be important to consider. Many of the various positions used by the Muslim in prayer may be strange to us, but they may all be identified in Scripture. We do not want to condone a ritualistic pattern of posture, nor do we wish to encourage a particular performance in prayer, but we could find that any one of these positions might be appropriate and helpful to adopt as the circumstances suit. We are free to worship God in whatever way seems right, as long as it is reverent and submissive. Nothing ought to stop us praying in a manner which is meaningful to our Muslim friend.

Muslims often engage in prayer by raising their hands in front of them, with their palms upward. In this country it has become associated with a certain group of Christians who are very demonstrative in their actions, and who take a particular line of teaching with respect to the Holy Spirit. Many Christians have understandably become suspicious of this particular action. Yet it ought to be recognised that it is a biblical way of coming into the presence of God: it appears that Moses prayed in a very similar manner (Exodus 17:11).

We may have further opportunities to show our Muslim friend we have yet more common areas of understanding, in which we may freely participate without fear of compromise. We too believe that God is one, that He is the sovereign Creator, and that He reveals His will to His people, etc. Let us pray for sanctified wisdom as we seek to win our Muslim brother or sister.

3. Establish Our Own Guidelines From Scripture
Do our Scriptures show us that *all* Muslim beliefs are entirely false? To answer this question we need to break down the beliefs that Muslims hold into their constituent parts and compare them with the word of God. Is it not possible to point to those aspects of the word that have a distinct parallel to what we find believed and practised in Islam? Taken as a whole Islam leads a person in a misguided direction; but many of the parts are not too far removed from what we believe, and may be used to point to a legitimate basis on which to build Bible truth. Let us look at one or two of these.

We need to be surrendered to God. To the Muslim this is a basic understanding and requirement. He cannot be a Muslim without considering his life in this way. He demonstrates it by his ritual practices (cf. Chapter 4). We ought to remember that this is what God requires of the believer in Christ. Our Scriptures plainly teach that the Christian life is one of total commitment through faith.

> **"Commit your way unto the Lord, trust also in Him."**   Psalm 37:5

> **"Trust in the Lord with all your heart, and lean not on your own understanding; in all your ways acknowledge Him, and He shall direct your paths."**
>   Proverbs 3:5-6

> **"I beseech you therefore, brethren, by the mercies of God, that you present your bodies a living sacrifice, holy, acceptable to God, which is your reasonable [rational/ spiritual] service."**
>   Romans 12:1

We have a simple credal statement. The Muslims have the *Shahada* (see Chapter 4 i.). We are used to the idea of the need for statements (or confessions) of faith to guide our thinking. However, these are usually relatively long declarations. Do we have anything to compare to the short and pithy Muslim statement, that sums up our faith in a concise way? Surely we might immediately think of the Apostle Paul's declaration concerning our Lord that

> **"God ... has highly exalted Him and given Him the name which is above every name, that at the name of Jesus every knee should bow ... and that every tongue should confess that *Jesus Christ is Lord*, to the glory of God the Father."**   Philippians 2:9-11

To be able to say with meaning and conviction that "**Jesus Christ is Lord**", as other New Testament writers explain, is an ability, privilege and responsibility that only those who are truly born again are able to undertake. It is both a prompting and an

enabling by the Holy Spirit. Therefore the Apostle John states in
a very similar vein:

> **"Whoever confesses that *Jesus is the Son of
> God*, God abides in him, and he in God."**
>
> 1 John 4:15

Our Lord Himself gave us a concise statement of faith by
defining eternal life in terms of knowing God and knowing
Himself:

> **"And this is eternal life, that they may know You, the
> only true God, and Jesus Christ whom You have
> sent."**   John 17:3

Here we have an explicit declaration concerning the One God,
Jesus his 'Apostle', or 'Sent One', and that eternal life is 'knowing God'. (This statement of Jesus does not deny his sonship,
although this may not be overtly contained within it). Notice the
similarity of style to that of the Muslim *Shahada* (cf. chapter 4:i.
p. 35)

We believe in the perfect revelation of God's will to mankind.
The revealed will of God shows us all that is necessary for us to
live for God in every aspect of life.

> **"From childhood you have known the Holy Scriptures
> which are able to make you wise for salvation through
> faith which is in Jesus Christ. All Scripture is given by
> inspiration of God, and is profitable for doctrine, for
> reproof, for correction, for instruction in righteous-
> ness, that the man of God may be complete, thoroughly
> equipped for every good work."**
>
> 2 Timothy 3:15-17

This quotation teaches us that we are to understand that the
whole of the written Scriptures we know as the *Holy Bible* are the

revelation of God's will to us. How do we know that our Scriptures are *truly* God's word? We believe God Himself has revealed the answer to this question to us also:

> **"Holy men of God spoke as they were moved by the Holy Spirit."**

By this the Apostle Peter seeks to emphasise the previous statement he makes, namely, that

> **"prophecy never came by the will of man . . ."**
> 2 Peter 1:21

We believe that obedience to the will of God as the expression of faith is the basic requirement for the people of God. Let us note the testimony of God's word:

> **"You will seek the Lord your God, and you will find Him if you seek Him with all your heart and with all your soul . . . When you turn to the Lord your God and obey His voice (for the Lord your God is a merciful God), He will not forsake you nor destroy you, nor forget the covenant of your fathers which He swore to them."**
> Deuteronomy 4:29-31

> **"By this we know that we know Him, if we keep His commandments . . . Whoever keeps His word, truly the love of God is perfected in him. By this we know that we are in Him . . . Whatever we ask we receive from Him, because we keep His commandments and do those things that are pleasing in His sight. And this is his commandment: that we should believe on the name of His Son Jesus Christ and love one another, as He gave us commandment . . . By this we know that we love the children of God, when we love God and keep His commandments. For this is the love of God, that we**

**keep His commandments. And His commandments
are not burdensome."**   1 John 2:3,5; 3:22,23; 5:2,3

*We are convinced that our Scriptures are perfectly adequate
and fully suited to meet the Muslim need.* The Muslim system is
one of legal requirement, of obtaining personal merit in order to
please God. However, we understand that salvation comes as a
free and sovereign gift of God. There is a great gulf between these
two views. They are in opposition to one another. To bridge the
gap is a major problem: that is beyond question. But it is not an
insurmountable problem. The Lord Jesus Christ addressed a very
similar dilemma. We read in the Gospel of John that:

**"the law was given by Moses, but grace and truth came
through Jesus Christ."**   John 1:17

Our Lord Himself highlights the pitfalls of our misusing the
law in his Sermon on the Mount, and leads us into a deeper
understanding of the need for a right attitude of heart and mind.
The Lord is often seen exposing hypocrisy, which is the result of
empty and meaningless law-keeping. Matthew 23 is worthy of
a detailed study on this aspect of our Lord's ministry. We may
again refer to that very telling parable which exposed the form of
classic self-righteousness that a system of law inspires:

**"He spoke this parable to some *who trusted in them-
selves* that they were righteous, and despised others:
'Two men went up to pray, one a Pharisee and the
other a tax collector. The Pharisee stood and prayed
thus with himself, "God, I thank You that I am not like
other men — extortioners, unjust, adulterers, or even
as this tax collector. I fast twice a week; I give tithes of
all that I possess." And the tax collector, standing afar
off, would not so much as raise his eyes to heaven, but
beat his breast, saying, "God be merciful to me a
sinner!" 'I tell you, this man went down to his house**

> **justified rather than the other; for everyone who
> exalts himself will be abased, and he who humbles
> himself will be exalted.'"**   Luke 18:9-14

4. Make use of the Scriptures

By now we are very much aware that our Muslim friends have problems of one sort or another in connection with our Scriptures, the Holy Bible. We must not be intimidated by this. There are again certain practical points that it would be wise for us to note.

Handle the Bible carefully. It is a holy book, and holds a special place in our lives. We must therefore take care that we handle our copy appropriately before the Muslim onlooker. We will not go to the lengths that he may with his Qur'an; but we ought to show our personal copy of the Holy Bible a deferential respect. Therefore we must not put it on the floor, nor place it on our laps! To do these things is offensive to the Muslim. He thinks that you are not caring what you do with God's word. Show that you do respect the fact that it is God's written word, and that it is no ordinary book to you. You will also find it helpful to refrain from using a marked and underlined Bible. It must not be thought that we are tampering with God's word in any way. We are not to be *'bibliolators'*, but we can be thoughtful and respectful about the manner in which we physically handle the written word of God.

Treat the Bible lovingly. It is the word of God, and it means a great deal to us. It is the revelation of the God of love: a God who desires to have a loving relationship with His people. If God gave His word to us through His love, and its pages demonstrate that love, then we ought to show our Muslim friend that it means as much to us. Let him see for himself, by the way we speak of it, that the Bible is the word of life to us.

Employ the Bible authoritatively. We must not be, or give the impression that we are, in any sense apologetic about the Bible. We do not need to argue its case or to defend it. Nor do we give the impression that we merely 'think' that it is God's word. Rather we must show that we know, and are convinced, it is God's word and that He is speaking to us through its written pages.

Utilise the Bible prayerfully. The Scriptures are not merely a text-book that we use to our advantage. We need to know and experience the power of the Holy Spirit in both interpreting and applying the word to the heart of our Muslim friend. We also need to know which aspects of teaching within the Scriptures are those that the Holy Spirit wants us to use on any particular occasion. Even if we have carefully planned out our discussion material beforehand, we need to be sensitive to the guidance of the Holy Spirit. We may be led not to use what we have prepared at all, or we may be directed to even more applicable Scriptures with respect to the situation and the receptiveness of the person with whom we are sharing these truths.

Our prayer must surely be, as we consider the practical implications of sharing the gospel in a meaningful and applicable manner to the Muslim, that

> **"you may be filled with the knowledge of His will in all wisdom and spiritual understanding; that you may lead a life worthy of the Lord, fully pleasing Him, being fruitful in every good work and increasing in the knowledge of God; strengthened with all might, according to His glorious power, for all patience and longsuffering with joy."**
> Colossians 1:9-11

10.
Making Known The Gospel Message (2)

We continue the principles begun in chapter 9.

5. Applying the Word of God
How can we show the Muslim the glory of Christ? This is surely one of the basic requirements of declaring the gospel. But is not the Muslim antagonistic before we even start to share Christ with him? That is true, but our extremely difficult task is not impossible! We must remember that nothing is impossible with God: He can overcome all mountains that stand in the way. He has given us this promise:

> **"Every valley shall be exalted, and every mountain shall be made low; the crooked places shall be made straight, and the rough places smooth; the glory of the Lord shall be revealed, and all flesh shall see it together; for the mouth of the Lord has spoken."**
> Isaiah 40:4,5

With the hope that this promise inspires in us we may go forward with confidence. We may take what can be called a somewhat indirect method.

We may approach the gospel by way of the Old Testament Scriptures. We have much in common with our Muslim friend here. He will find that he has a great affinity for what he finds there, and it may generate a remarkable curiosity. We must never forget that in the Old Testament we have the foundation of the gospel of salvation through the Lord Jesus Christ: it is the record of God's own preparation for the sending of the Son of His love

to be the final and complete sacrifice for sin. As it is a means of
preparation in itself we can prepare our Muslim friends by using
it. All we are doing, then, is to pursue God's own preparation
method!

We may look first at the *Torah* (which Muslims refer to as the
Taurat), the five books of Moses. According to a Qur'anic
injunction every Muslim ought to accept and know them. The
Pentateuch, as we more commonly refer to these books of Moses,
demonstrates God's sovereign power and authority and testifies
of God as creator and guide of his people. These Scriptures
explain the entrance of sin, identify what sin is, and describe
God's gracious provision of salvation to Noah.

They relate God's dealings with Abraham and his family, and
show how they become the people of God. The law is given as
instruction to God's people, to show them how to live appropriately before Him. Its purpose is clearly summed up in the
following quotation:

> "Hear, O Israel: the Lord our God, the Lord is one!
> You shall love the Lord your God with all your heart,
> with all your soul, and with all your might. And these
> words which I command you today shall be in your
> heart; you shall teach them diligently to your children,
> and shall talk of them when you sit in your house, when
> you walk by the way, when you lie down, and when you
> rise up. You shall bind them as a sign on your hand,
> and they shall be as frontlets between your eyes. You
> shall write them on the doorposts of your house and on
> your gates."   Deuteronomy 6:4-9

The *Psalms* (the Muslim *Zabur*) are a wellspring of teaching
on the godly life. They show clearly many elements of the life
that is pleasing to God. For example, Psalm 1 is very suitable to
use with a Muslim: for it shows the contrast between the godly life
and the life of the ungodly.

The *Proverbs* are a valuable repository of faithful and wise sayings that have a great appeal to the Muslim mind. They are a collection of psychologically sound and practical pieces of advice on relationships in every area of life. First and foremost they address our relationship with God, working out into the family, and to the community at large.

The *Prophets*. Our Muslim friend believes in the prophets, so we may show how God spoke through them. In doing so we shall highlight the disobedience of His chosen people, demonstrating how impossible it was for them to keep the law. We may also point out that the prophets are messengers of hope, of good news to come, for they spoke of one whom God would send, His anointed Servant, the Messiah: One who was to be a Son, who would come to save His people, and give them a glorious future in His kingdom.

There are various ways we may help our Muslim friend to understand the truths of Scripture. There is no single guaranteed method. We must continually trust in the leading of the Holy Spirit to give us wisdom in this matter. We must recognise that the Holy Spirit may well be inspiring the particular line of questioning that comes from our Muslim enquirer, when it comes from the heart with sincerity and seriousness. We must take great care not to be drawn into controversy. It is usually totally non-productive to argue our beliefs, and often proves very destructive. Such a situation will effectively demonstrate that there is no basis of trust or respect either from the Muslim to us, or vice versa. We will not be able to make any progress if we get ourselves in that position.

As we are now at the point of introducing the Lord Jesus Christ to our Muslim enquirer, it is important to consider how we may refer to Him without giving offence, or ending the relationship that we have worked at for so long. We know the Lord Jesus Christ is *the Son of God*. This is an important theological concept that is clearly and demonstrably taught in the Scriptures. Yet, as we relate to the Muslim, it is wise not to use the term, at least, until we have developed some understanding of what it really means. The Muslim already has in mind what he thinks we mean by it, and if we listen to him we will discover that his idea is a totally blasphemous one (see Chapter 8 on 'Trinity'). Does this mean that we might be undermining Scripture by not using this expression? Many suspect that if we avoid using this title, we are undermining Christ's position and authority. It *is* a fundamental doctrine, and to avoid its use must surely mean that we are detracting from both His person and work. But is this really the case?

Let us observe how the Lord refers to Himself:

> **"The high priest answered and said to Him [Jesus], 'I adjure You by the living God that You tell us if You are the Christ [the Messiah], the Son of God.' Jesus said to him, 'It is as you said. Nevertheless, I say to you, hereafter you will see the Son of Man sitting at the right hand of the Power, and coming on the clouds of heaven.'"**
> Matthew 26:63,64

Jesus did not deny that He was the Son of God; He affirmed it by saying, "It is as you said". Nevertheless, as so often elsewhere in the Gospels, when speaking of Himself, Jesus prefers to use the title 'Son of Man'. In Mark 8:31, for instance we read,

> **"He [Jesus] began to teach them that the Son of Man must suffer many things ..."**

We therefore have our Lord's own example to follow. It is worth studying the balance in the Gospels between the theological truth that Jesus *is* the Son of God, and the way that He presented Himself to a people who would be greatly offended at the term *'Son of God'*. It is *not* dishonest, or misleading, or even compromise, to try to find alternative inoffensive ways of speaking about our Lord Jesus Christ.

When talking with Muslims it is not wise to speak merely of

'Jesus', for that is not reverent to Muslim ears (is it reverent even to Christian ears?). We ought to speak of the *Lord Jesus, Jesus the Messiah, Jesus the Word, the Lord Jesus Christ*. There are other biblical titles that we are at liberty to use with great effect also. By doing so we may bring all the truth that there is behind the phrase 'Son of God' into those terms. We may use the title 'Son of God' eventually when our Muslim friend understands that we do *not* mean by it a human generation: a misconception which is, as we have seen, as much blasphemy to us as it is to him. We ought therefore to feel strongly in a positive way on this issue.

Let us consider some further means that we may use to help our Muslim enquirer to understand biblical truth.

When we turn to the *New Testament* we may be able to use the Gospel *parables* systematically to great effect. Our Lord gave us the parables to explain important truths in a graphic manner, but He also used them to express spiritual truth. If stated simply in an unveiled form such truths may be received with suspicion, offence and misunderstanding. The parables are therefore not merely illustrations of truths, but may be thought of in a more positive way. They constitute a cultural method of teaching by which truths that are difficult to assimilate are presented in concrete form, and therefore become more understandable and acceptable. We must bear in mind that they were spoken to Jewish audiences, and may need some exposition to make them relevant to the Muslim mind and experience. However, we do have a great advantage in the fact that they were originally given in a Middle Eastern context, and are therefore already relevant to the way of thinking of our Muslim friend.

Bearing all this in mind we must conclude that we may legitimately use the parables to teach the fundamental truths of the gospel to Muslim people. Here is a suggestion as to how they may be used to illustrate gospel truth.

Concerning Sin:

Luke 18:9-14	The Pharisee and the tax collector.
Luke 12:16-21	The rich fool.

Matthew 15:1-20 Ceremonial and real defilement compared.
Concerning God's Love and Mercy, together with our need for repentance:

Luke 15:3-7	The lost sheep.
Luke 15:8-10	The lost coin.
Luke 15:11-32	The lost son.

Concerning the Judgement of God:

Matthew 13:24-30	The wheat and the weeds.
Matthew 13:47-50	The fishing net.

Concerning God's Plan for Man's Salvation:

Matthew 22:1-14	The wedding banquet (emphasising the need for righteousness).
Luke 20:9-18	The vineyard tenants (showing how God sent his Son and how He was rejected).

Concerning the Cost of Discipleship in Following Christ:

Matthew 13:44	Hidden treasure.
Matthew 13:45-46	A precious pearl.
Luke 6:48-49	The wise and foolish builders.

Concerning Christian Living and Stewardship:

Matthew 18:23-35	The unmerciful servant (on forgiveness).
Luke 7:41-43	The two debtors (on forgiving others).
Luke 12:42-48	The faithful servant (on serving God).
Luke 19:11-27	The gold coins (talents) (on serving God).
Luke 5:36-39	New cloth, new wine (on the fact that the way of Christ is completely new).
Luke 10:25-37	The good Samaritan (on love).

There is a booklet entitled *"Parables of the Lord Jesus"*, published by *Scripture Gift Mission*, which presents them topically and in a way which can profitably be used with Muslims. Let us look at their arrangement in detail. The parables are systematically arranged under seven headings:

God is speaking:	The sower
	The two builders
	The good neighbour
	The rich fool
The Saviour is seeking:	The lost sheep
	The lost coin
	The lost son
The need to repent and believe:	
	The barren fruit tree
	The proud man and the repentant man
The need to forgive:	The unforgiving servant
The need to be ready:	The ten bridesmaids
The invitation:	The great supper
The judgement:	The wedding garment
	The wicked vinedressers
	The fishing net

Interspersed among these parables are other texts and passages of Scripture which explain the way of salvation more explicitly. The booklet ends with a separate section entitled '*Now is the day of salvation*', using verses that relate our Lord's own claims as Saviour. The booklet is very helpful in the way it presents its message in a sensitive yet direct way and sets a good example for us.

If we do have the opportunity to meet with a Muslim enquirer on a regular basis, and he has the desire to examine Christian teaching in a serious way, then we need to consider a programme that will present the gospel message systematically. We ought to devise a plan that starts with the less controversial subjects on which we have some common ground of contact, but which are nonetheless very important doctrinally. Some ten subjects are suggested which would be valuable in such a scheme.[1]

i) *God is One, and has created Man to serve and love Him.* The Ten Commandments begin with an outright condemnation of idolatry: Exodus 20:3-5. This identifies with the Muslim

concept of *Shirk*, the sin of associating anything created with God
the Creator. Here we have a definitive reason why the Muslim
will never entertain the idea of having pictures of Mohammed: he
takes this command quite literally. We may go on to emphasise
the need for obedience to the one God: Deuteronomy 6:1-7. A
strong emphasis needs to be put on complete personal commitment to God.

Jesus the Messiah gives his own approval to this teaching,
and is very positive in expressing it: Mark 12:29-30. The Apostle
Paul is often accused by Muslims of corrupting the pure teaching
of the real gospel, thereby causing Christians to associate others
with the one God. In answer to this we would refer to his first
letter to the Corinthian Church to corroborate the united testimony of Scripture:

> **"Therefore concerning the eating of things of-
> fered to idols, we know that an idol is nothing in
> the world, and that there is no other God but one.
> For even if there are so-called gods, whether in
> heaven or on earth (as there are many gods and
> many lords), yet for us there is only one God, the
> Father, of whom are all things, and we live for
> Him; and one Lord Jesus Christ, through whom
> are all things, and through whom we live."**
>
> 1 Corinthians 8:4-6

There is also his very explicit declaration to Timothy:

> **"For there is one God and one mediator between
> God and men, the man Christ Jesus."**
>
> 1 Timothy 2:5

The Apostle specifically and outrightly condemns idolatry:
Galatians 5:19-21. John includes idolatry among the sins which
deserve the condemnation of hell: Revelation 21:8. We may also
refer back to the Psalms that give a call to worship the one God

who has revealed Himself through His mighty acts of creation
and throughout history: Psalm 33:1,4-9; 105:1-6. We might particularly note the prayers of worship which express the believer's
joy and thankfulness, his reverence for God, and his confidence
in Him as a personal God: Psalm 95:1-7; 139:1-6,13,14.

ii) *God has given His laws to Man.*

We here refer back to the Ten Commandments to show that
we cannot know what sin is unless we know the standards that
God has set: Exodus 20:1-17. As we examine these and apply
them to our lives we begin to realise just how far short we have
fallen. We are able to show the various ways in which Jesus the
Messiah based much of his teaching on these revealed laws. He
summarised their demands in terms of loving God and loving our
neighbour: Matthew 22:34-40. Our Lord plainly demonstrates
that the law not only applies to our outward actions, but also to our
inner thoughts and motives: Matthew 5:21-24,27,28. He shows
us that God's standards are so much higher than the moral
standards of every human society: Matthew 5:43-45.

We may also turn to Psalm 119 and point out how the
psalmist believes that the basic desire of the true believer is to
surrender himself completely and utterly to God, and to a dedicated obedience of His revealed will.

iii) *God warns Man of the consequences of failure to keep His
laws.*

The record of Adam and Eve in Genesis 2-3 is fundamentally
relevant. The entrance of sin brings a sense of shame to man, and
activates his conscience so that he realises that he is spiritually
naked before a holy God. We must carefully teach that every man
and woman is responsible before God for all their actions:
Ezekiel 18:1-4,30-32. The emphasis here is clearly that each
individual is responsible for his own sins. The Scriptures
consistently testify of the desperate and dreadful nature of sin.
Romans 3:9-20,23, by way of example, emphasises sin's univer-
sality and power, and teaches that it is a rebellion against God, and

not merely a making of mistakes through inherent moral weakness. The basic requirement that must be recognised is that each person needs to acknowledge and confess his sinfulness and to return to God by means of a genuine repentance: Psalm 51:1-9.

iv) *God is merciful and forgives.*
We may now be able to introduce the concept of the '*Fatherhood*' of God in terms of Psalm 103:8-14. This doctrine is foreign to the Muslim, yet it should not present any major problem as we take care to explain that God is the one who is the origin of all life, and that He gives us life.

God has decreed, from the depths of eternity past, that He will deal with man's sin by means of sacrifice. This sacrifice must be understood in terms of the giving of a perfect life in the place of the sinful life to pay the penalty of sin. Justice must be done so that God's perfect righteousness and holiness are perfectly and legally vindicated. We must teach very clearly that God cannot look upon sin, and therefore cannot accept the sinner without his sin being atoned. By means of a just atonement God's anger against sin can be turned away from the sinner. These truths can be taught from Leviticus 9:7; 16:5-10,21-22. Here we especially note that forgiveness is not a matter of mere words, but that there is a tremendous cost, a high price in real terms, to pay. From Jeremiah 5:7,9 and Hosea 11:8-9 we can open up the question of how God forgives, and point to this need for atonement. We may then turn again to the Psalms, to see something of the joy there is in knowing that one's sins are truly forgiven: Psalm 32:1-7.

v) *God revealed to the prophets that He would come among men.*
The doctrine of the incarnation may be introduced through relevant Old Testament passages which speak of God *Himself* coming to live among men. He comes *in* His word: Isaiah 55:10-11. It can be demonstrated that first the tabernacle, and later the temple, were intended as signs of God's presence: His dwelling in the midst of His people: Exodus 29:44-45; Leviticus

26:1,2,11,12; Ezekiel 37:26,27. God personally declares that He is coming to reveal Himself, to make Himself known in truth, and to proclaim His covenant: Isaiah 40:3-5. The believer, who recognises that God is coming to establish justice and His kingdom on earth, experiences real joy and boldness through confidence in God: Psalm 96:1-10. In Isaiah 64:1-9 we have a prayer that God will come as He has promised to reveal Himself and show mercy to sinful and rebellious man.

vi) *God sent Jesus the Messiah as His Word by means of a miraculous birth, and gave Him miraculous powers.*

Under this section we may look first at the accounts of the birth of Jesus the Messiah: Matthew 1:18-25; Luke 2:1-20. We have to admit that most details of His childhood and earlier life have not been recorded, but we have a great deal of evidence to show the uniqueness of His life during the record of His ministry. Three particular miracles are helpful to point this out, from differing angles. The *stilling of the storm*, showing the reaction of His disciples, demonstrates that their faith in Him grew gradually: Luke 8:22-25. The narrative of the *feeding of the five thousand* is helpful in the light of the Qur'anic passage, in which Jesus the Messiah is asked:

> "Is thy Lord able to send down for us a table spread with food from Heaven?"   Qur'an: Sura 5: 112-115

The *casting out of the unclean spirit* shows the power that the Lord exercised over all forces of evil: Luke 4:31-37.

vii) *God gave Jesus the Messiah the message of the Injil (gospel) to proclaim.*

We are given brief summaries of the gospel message in the words of Jesus himself: Mark 1:14,15; Luke 5:17-26. It ought to be borne in mind that although the Qur'an indicates an understanding that the *Injil* (the gospel) was granted to Jesus the Messiah no content is given to it, and it becomes a nebulous

entity. This is our opportunity to share its real message. The
particular value of the latter passage is that it draws attention to
what Jesus actually did: He healed the sick man and at the very
same time declared his sins to be forgiven. Do not be surprised
if our Muslim friend reacts as the Pharisee did! We may point out
however that our understanding of this truth is not drawn from the
later writings of Paul and the Apostles; that it is not merely an
interpretation of what happened, but is truly based on what Jesus
did and said.

The parable of *the prodigal son*, Luke 15:11-32, emphasises
that God's forgiveness is based on His love for the sinner, and that
the relationship of the one forgiven is not the status of slave, as
the Muslim maintains, but rather is that of a son. The Lord's
Prayer, Matthew 6:9-13, shows how Jesus encouraged his disciples to pray to God as sons addressing a loving Father. This is
a valuable and necessary aspect of teaching to introduce to a
Muslim, and must be undertaken with care to avoid misunderstandings.

viii) *God demonstrates His love for sinners through the death
of Jesus the Messiah.*

This subject is one of the most difficult to discuss with a
Muslim. His prejudices against the concept are very deep-seated.
Nevertheless, we must seek to place it in the context of the love
of God. It is probably wise to consider the reasons why God
expressed His love in this way, before considering the details of
the event itself. The Muslim *does not deny* that the Jews wanted
to kill Jesus; nor that Jesus was *willing* to be killed. He *denies
only that God allowed Jesus the Messiah to be crucified.*

Appropriate parts of the Gospel narrative ought to be pointed
out carefully. We must show something of the hostility of the
Jews against Jesus the Messiah: John 5:15-18. Point out His
willingness to be captured and killed: Luke 22:41-44. He laid
down his own life voluntarily: He was not forced to do so: He
knew that the Father in heaven could have rescued Him from
death if that had been His will: Matthew 26:51-54. Show how the

Jews finally decided to kill Jesus: Luke 22:66-23:2. We need to be aware that the Muslim is likely to react in a very similar way to the Jews in the charge of blasphemy against the Lord Jesus Christ.

We may then go on to look at a straightforward account of the actual crucifixion, such as we find in Luke 23:20-26. It is important to understand all that happens in the light of the prophecy concerning the Suffering Servant who bears the sins of men: Isaiah 53:4-6. In this context the prayer of the psalmist recorded in Psalm 22:1-9 is very meaningful. This is the prayer of one who feels that God has rejected and abandoned him. His utterances become the very words Jesus used on the cross. His prayer was heard and answered: He was not rescued before His death, but after death. Through His death He broke the power of death and cancelled the debt of sin.

ix) *God raised Jesus the Messiah from death to life.*

We come now to consider the empty tomb and the appearances of the risen Messiah: Luke 23:50-56; 24:1-12. The record of the two disciples who met the Lord on the Emmaus road is particularly helpful, for here Jesus the Messiah explains in person the necessity of His suffering and death: Luke 24:13-35. Further appearances to His disciples consolidate the eye-witness account: Luke 24:36-47. Hebrews 2:14-18 is a useful commentary on the necessity of the death and resurrection of the Messiah: demonstrating how He was one with us, having experienced the same temptations as we do; how He suffered physically, and experienced death like us. It was because He endured these things that He is able to sympathise with us when we face them. As He both faced and overcame all the powers of evil, we believe He is able to help us to do the same. Because He died, Jesus the Messiah has broken the hold that death once had over men and women.

The Gospel record clearly states that Jesus the Messiah is raised up from the grave, and given resurrection life. His resurrection is the vindication of both His integrity and His

obedience to the will of His heavenly Father: Ephesians 1:20-21;
Romans 1:4; Colossians 2:12. His resurrection consequently
brings hope to every believer, that, like Him, he too will be raised
to the same resurrection life.

The psalmist expressed the confidence the believer has that
there is life beyond death: Psalm 16:1-11. It is a resurrection life
in which we have the ultimate joy of being in the actual presence
of God himself. How different this is from the Muslim concept
of paradise as portrayed in the Qur'an.

x) *God gave His Spirit to the disciples who acknowledged
Jesus as God's Messiah and God's Word.*

In the first two chapters of *Acts* there is a great deal of valuable
teaching about the relationship of the Holy Spirit to Jesus the
Messiah, and how He first came to the disciples, the close
followers of Jesus the Messiah. The tremendous impact that this
had on them is described. Peter's sermon in Acts 2 expresses the
relationship between God, the Lord Jesus, and the Holy Spirit, in
the simple terms in which the Early Church was to understand it.

The work of the Holy Spirit is particularly described in
Romans 8:1-17. Paul the Apostle clearly establishes that Man is
unable to help himself spiritually, although he thinks he can. This
latter thought is a notion that is in line with Muslim optimism.
God's provision for Man in his fallen sinful nature includes the
incarnation, atonement and the granting of the Holy Spirit to
enable believers to obey His law. It is because the work of God's
Spirit takes place in the heart, that believers are able to know God
as their heavenly Father. It is here that our discussion about Jesus
being the Son of God may be taken out of the area of controversy
and placed into the context of our experience of God.

Psalm 51 is a very expressive prayer of penitence. It is the
confession of a heart that is overwhelmed by shame; humbled and
broken by a sense of guilt. It is also a clear statement of faith,
confidence and hope in the mercy of God. Note in particular
vv.10-17. If our Muslim friend could express himself in these
terms in and through the name of our Lord Jesus Christ we would

be very hopeful that he might be coming to experience, or even have already received, God's saving grace. It is surely our prayer that our friend may show such true repentance and faith. We long for him to believe that it is only through Jesus that we can enjoy this kind of a relationship with God.

****

Please note that the suggestions made in this chapter are meant only to be a guide. There is available a certain amount of other helpful material that could be used to explain our faith to Muslims. The author personally worked on a foreign language Bible Correspondence School programme in which he found it profitable to divide the total study curriculum for Muslims into four sections, as follows: (i) a general course on the contents of the Books of Moses, the Psalms and the Prophets, following the progressive revelation of God's plan for salvation in the Old Testament. (ii) 'Jesus the Messiah': a course specifically on the life of Christ as narrated through the Gospels. (iii) 'God's Way': this was compiled from a set of papers written by a born-again Muslim national, and discussed (not argued) various theological topics of particular interest to Muslims that were covered in the previous two courses. It sought to consolidate the truths presented in the first two courses, and considered their implications. (iv) 'The Way of Salvation' was a translation of 'Right with God' by John Blanchard (published by Banner of Truth Trust). This volume, it was believed, presented the gospel in terms that might be acceptable to a Muslim. Chapter 1 was not used as that deals with arguments for the Bible being the word of God. It was felt that it was right to begin with that assumption, as the students had already been using Scripture with this understanding. The rest of the book presented the gospel message and employed very appropriate Scriptures for use with Muslims. The last chapter ('The Way Ahead') was expanded with helpful material to encourage the new believer, and give him practical help to know how to live sensitively as a Christian in a Muslim environment.

A published course that takes a similar approach is one produced in Africa. It is in the form of four booklets with the following titles:

(i) "The Beginning of People": 'Lessons from the First Book of the Taurat of the Prophet Moses';

(ii) "God's Covenant with the People of Israel": 'Lessons from the Second Book of the Taurat of the Prophet Moses, Zabur of the Prophet David, and Other Prophets of God';

(iii) "God Loves People": 'Lessons from The Injil of Jesus the Messiah';

(iv) "The People of God": 'More Lessons from The Holy Scriptures'. This last booklet deals with the Church as portrayed in Acts and discusses aspects of the practical Christian life, quoting from Matthew through to Revelation.

This course is published by Evangel Publishing House, P.O. Box 1015, Kisumu, Kenya. It is a very appropriate approach, sharing with a Muslim very simply the teaching of the Holy Bible.

This general review of approaches to Muslim enquirers and contacts is presented in the hope that it might be of assistance in showing the direction it is profitable to take in thinking through a faithful presentation of the truths of the word of God. It is our prayerful concern that the gospel may be presented as appropriate opportunities arise, and that this may be done in a helpful and relevant manner, addressing the particular problems that are presented by our Muslim friend. We must present the gospel message authoritatively and sensitively, praying that the Holy Spirit will give understanding of the truth as it is in our Lord Jesus Christ. May we have the privilege of seeing the promise of God given through the prophet Ezekiel worked out with respect to the Muslim with whom we are concerned:

> **"I will give you a new heart and put a new spirit within you; I will take the heart of stone out of your flesh and give you a heart of flesh. I will**

> put My Spirit within you and cause you to walk
> in My statutes, and you will keep My judgments
> and do them ... You shall be My people, and I
> will be your God."
>
> Ezekiel 36:26-28

1. *The subsequent outline is based on a series of passages of
   Scripture that have been published as a pamphlet by the Bible
   Society in Lebanon (in English, French and Arabic) entitled
   "The Message of the Tawrat, the Zabur and the Injil - Selected
   Passages from the Holy Bible." In his book 'You Go And Do
   The Same', Colin Chapman gives a very helpful study based
   on the same source, and it is recommended for consideration.*

Part II

Conclusion

As *"ambassadors for Christ"* (2 Corinthians 5:20) we have been given the *"ministry of reconciliation"* (v.18). This is a God-given responsibility to show sinners the way to obtain true righteousness. We need to apply ourselves to the task of pointing the way to a positive relationship with God, and the road to salvation. The Apostle demonstrates the attitude we are to have to this duty:

> **"We are ambassadors for Christ, as though God were pleading through us: we implore you on Christ's behalf, be reconciled to God. For He made Him who knew no sin to be sin for us, that we might become the righteousness of God in Him."**   2 Corinthians 5:20-21

The first chapter (Sura) of the Qur'an is a prayer that the Muslim recites every time he comes formally to pray, as well as on many other occasions. The words are very meaningful to him, and he says them very fervently:

> "Praise be to God, the Lord of Creation,
> The Compassionate, the Merciful, King of Judgement Day!
> You alone we worship, and to You alone we pray for help.
> Guide us to (show us) the straight path,

The path of those whom You have favoured (blessed).
Not of those who have incurred Your wrath,
Nor of those who have gone astray". (Qur'an: Sura 1)
This is the cry from a Muslim heart. Do we not have the
answer to this prayer?

> **"There is a way which seems right to a man, but
> its end is the way of death."** Proverbs 14:12
> **"All we like sheep have gone astray; we have
> turned, every one, to his own way."** Isaiah 53:6
> **"Jesus said, 'I am the good shepherd. The good
> shepherd gives His life for the sheep.'"**
> John 10:11
> **"Jesus said, 'I am the way, the truth, and the life.
> No man comes to the Father except through
> Me.'"** John 14:6
> **"Enter by the narrow gate; for wide is the gate
> and broad is the way that leads to destruction,
> and there are many who go in by it. Because
> narrow is the gate and difficult is the way which
> leads to life, and there are few who find it."**
> Matthew 7:13,14
> **"The Lord is my shepherd, I shall not want . . .
> He restores my soul; He leads me in the paths of
> righteousness for His name's sake."** Psalm 23:1,3

It is admittedly not proving to be an easy task to reach
Muslims for Christ, but we trust that we have demonstrated from
Scripture that it is not an impossibility. The Muslim has a very
high view of God, though it is misplaced and misdirected. We
have an even higher view of the sovereignty of God: of the one
true God who reaches down in love and mercy in the person of the
Lord Jesus Christ to save sinners who are unable to help themselves. The Muslim is in fact wonderfully open to the gospel
message when all the misunderstandings are removed. You will
find that he is usually very willing to talk with you about the

gospel. Let us therefore take every opportunity that is presented to us so that we may share the word of God boldly and fearlessly with the Muslim, in the enabling power and wisdom granted us by the Holy Spirit.

There have been many examples in history to demonstrate the Muslim's antipathy to the gospel, but let us take care how we react to what we have heard and been led to believe. In closing it may be good to consider a recent assessment of the task:

> "There is, of course, the biblical command to shake the dust from our feet and go elsewhere when a people reject the gospel. *Nevertheless, most Muslims have never explicitly rejected the gospel.* Their apparent resistance is usually related to the fact that they have never understood its message. An apparently resistant people are not necessarily a people who have rejected. In fact I have seldom interacted with any other people who seem as open to hearing the gospel as Muslims. Nevertheless, the misperceptions run deep, the theological issues are profound, and community pressures are tremendous. It takes time. *Patience is required*, the kind of patience which does not fit the categories of any forms of cost effectiveness and analysis. It is patience born out of commitment to Jesus Christ who also lived among a people who often painfully misunderstood his ministry."
>
> (Shenk 1983: 153 (N.B.: Italics mine))

Let us therefore consider a thorough-going and well thought-through biblical presentation of the gospel of Christ that we may take to the Muslim. He is not outside the scope of our understanding or an appropriate application of the glorious gospel of the sovereign grace of God.

Women in Islam

As soon as one begins to refer to women in Islam and Muslim attitudes towards them, one is aware of the tremendous amount of feeling that is engendered in the western world, especially among evangelical Christians. The place of women in the Christian church is itself a very warm issue. It is true to say that in recent years the role of women in the Christian family and in the life of the church has been given a much greater balance than has previously been the case, though there is a strong tendency to tip that balance into something other than biblical. This needs to be mentioned because we inevitably see the status of women in Islam in the light of our western cultural experience, and what many consider to have been the inexcusable way Christian women were treated in the Victorian era.

Bearing this in mind, an appeal is made that we look at the subject, not with our own cultural bias, nor by any imposition of what *we* may think the place of women in *our* society ought to be. It would be more profitable to consider the Muslim view of women in the light of the Scriptures.

1. A Biblical Foundation

In Christian thought, women are equal in person and character to men. Both man and woman have a parallel identity and equality before God. However, we recognise men and women have different roles and different responsibilities in Christian society. The creation ordinance points to the responsibility and privilege of woman to be a helpmeet to man, to complement him, and bring a balance to his life.

"Then the rib which the LORD God had taken from

man He made into a woman, and He brought her to the
man. And Adam said: 'This is now bone of my bones
and flesh of my flesh; She shall be called Woman,
because she was taken out of Man.' Therefore a man
shall leave his father and mother and be joined to his
wife, and they shall become one flesh."

Genesis 2:22-24

Another important aspect that is inherent in this passage, and
can be clearly understood from the way that God created both
man and woman, is that woman has a particular responsibility in
child-bearing. This was made more difficult and painful because
of the entrance of sin into the world, and its judgement.

"To the woman He [God] said: 'I will greatly
multiply your sorrow and your conception; in
pain you shall bring forth children; your desire
shall be for your husband, and he shall rule over
you."

Genesis 3:16

The scriptural view of woman is that she has an important role
in the family and in society, both of which would suffer if she did
not fulfil her God-given responsibility. It is a role that is different
from that of man, but it must never be considered inferior.
Another obvious truth that is clearly understood from the above
cited passages is that man has a distinct authority to exercise.
Adam demonstrated it as he fulfilled God's command in naming
'Woman' (Genesis 1:28, cf 2:19,20,23). In all this it must be
remembered that both man and woman are equally created in the
image of God.

"God created man in His own image; in the
image of God He created him; male and female
He created them."

Genesis 1: 27

We are seeking only to lay a biblical foundation concerning
the Christian view of women. We are not attempting an in-depth

discussion. Yet we cannot ignore one very important theological passage in the New Testament on this subject. The Apostle Paul, though misunderstood by some to be a misogynist, is at great pains, under the constraint of the Holy Spirit, to express truth in the noblest manner.

> **"Wives, submit to your own husbands, as to the Lord. For the husband is head of the wife, as also Christ is head of the church; and He is the Saviour of the body. Therefore, just as the church is subject to Christ, so let the wives be to their own husbands in everything.**
>
> **Husbands, love your wives, just as Christ also loved the church and gave Himself for it, that He might sanctify and cleanse it with the washing of water by the word, that He might present it to Himself a glorious church, not having spot or wrinkle or any such thing, but that it should be holy and without blemish. So husbands ought to love their own wives as their own bodies; he who loves his wife loves himself. For no one ever hated his own flesh, but nourishes and cherishes it, just as the Lord does the church.**
>
> **For we are members of His body, of His flesh and of His bones. 'For this reason a man shall leave his father and mother and be joined to his wife, and the two shall become one flesh.' This is a great mystery, but I speak concerning Christ and the church. Nevertheless let each one you in particular so love his own wife as himself, and let the wife see that she respects her husband."**

Ephesians 5:22-33

Can there be any greater incentive to make sure that the role of man and woman is kept in a right and noble balance? There is respect, acceptance and special regard for the various and differing roles of man and woman. Do we see this truly transcendent view of the relationship between man and woman in the western expression of the evangelical Christian church? If we are to answer truthfully, we surely have to admit that we fail to maintain such a noble pattern. Can we then be honest enough to confess that we fall short of our own biblical standard? Would it be too strong to say that instead of getting up on our 'high horse' of righteous criticism and indignation with respect to our evaluation of the place of women in Islam, we ought rather to follow our Lord's example where He was faced with a specific moral question:

> **"He who is without sin among you, let him throw a stone at her first."**   John 8:7

Let us therefore turn to consider the subject of the place of women in Islam in a sensitive, caring and compassionate manner. We have deliberately taken this line of thought so that we are not unthinkingly or harshly critical of situations outside our immediate experience. Yet it has not been presented so that we may think more favourably of the way women in Islam are treated. We are merely making the point that we are often harsh in our assessment of others, but have a distinct tendency to be more than lenient with ourselves! The reason we began this way is that we might consider the subject of 'women in Islam' from a more reasonable and realistic perspective. We need to think of their situation with sympathy, compassion, understanding, and kind-heartedness, in the light of God's word and truth, and not with the limitations and attitudes governed by personal prejudice.

2. The Qur'anic View of Women

Mohammed's own personal attitude to women has been something approaching a scandal to Christians. While in no way wishing to explain away the problem that Mohammed's conduct is to us, we must attempt to consider it with some degree of impartiality. We must point out in the first place that Mohammed married the widow Khadijah, many years his senior, and on her own initiative(!), when he was twenty-five years old. He remained faithful to her until she died, and did not marry anyone else during the period of this marriage - some twenty-five years. This detail is emphasised in a great deal of Muslim literature relating to Mohammed's life. His marriage was considered a happy one, and they had six children: two boys, who died during childhood, and four girls.

Muslims are deeply sensitive about their prophet's private life and his attitude to women during his later years. Many historians tend to gloss over, or even ignore, some of these problems. They seek to emphasise his numerous exploits and to show that he exerted all his energies in the establishing of the Muslim community in troublesome circumstances.

Soon after Khadija's death Mohammed married Sawdah, 30 years of age, and an early convert to Islam. It is maintained that Mohammed saw in her a *spiritual* companion to replace the encouragement and support that his beloved Khadijah had brought to him, and which he now deeply missed. It has also been suggested that the marriage may have been more of a political expedient. Sawdah's previous husband had been a close follower of Mohammed, but had died. As Mohammed was head of what was then a small band of Muslims, it is suggested that he might have considered marriage with Sawdah a prudent measure which avoided having to marry her to someone outside the group (it must be remembered that a woman had no security outside a marriage arrangement, and might well be left destitute). One supportive statement for this view argues on the basis of Mohammed's mature years and heavy responsibility:

> "As for Muhammad himself there are signs that deepening religious experiences were taking the place of human companionship."   (Watt 1980: 79)

Two years later another marriage is reported to have been 'consummated' with A'ishah in April 623. She had the 'distinction' of being only nine years of age, and Mohammed is reported to have joined in her child-play. In this case it is argued that the relationship between a 53 year old man and a girl of nine or ten must necessarily have been more like that of father and daughter.

> "Her marriage was clearly for the political reason of binding together Abu-Bakr and Muhammad, and just as Abu-Bakr was Muhammad's chief lieutenant, so she was his chief wife, even though three years earlier after the death of Khadijah he had married Sawdah, a Muslim widow of about thirty."   (Watt 1980: 102)

It is not appropriate for us to enter into an in-depth study of Mohammed's marriages, but we must note what we are being asked to believe. We are informed that most of Mohammed's marriages, as well as those of his daughters and close Muslim associates

> "are found to have political reasons of one kind or another."   (Watt 1980: 102-3)

Another author appeals quite forcefully that Mohammed's motives should not be misunderstood! He sets forth the argument that a fifty year old man as involved in establishing political ideals as Mohammed was, does not get married for the same pleasure one expects that a twenty-five year old would experience through it.

> "Even if the Prophet had married a number of women, as a normal Arab of his day did, there would be nothing morally repugnant about this providing a sense of proportion was kept . . . Given the right conditions monogamy is certainly the ideal form . . . The Qur'an, therefore, laid down monogamy as the moral law for long-term achievement, but permitted polygamy immediately as a legal solution of the situation. Indeed, in Arabia conditions were in a way even worse than in the post-war West, the common factor being a disproportionate decrease in the

> number of men as compared to women chiefly due to
> wars, for in the West the woman is economically inde-
> pendent and in any case there is some form of social
> insurance."
> (Rahman 1979: 29)

This leads us on to consider the teaching of the Qur'an on the
place and status of women in general. Interestingly, the Qur'an
has more to say on the standing of women than on any other social
question.

The condition of women in the Arabia of Mohammed's day
had been very low indeed. A woman was not an object of great
respect. Mohammed sought to make some amends for their
degradation and dishonour. To that end he established new
principles on how women were to be both treated and considered.
His reforms, as far as they went, actually enhanced to a considerable degree the status of women in Arabia. However, the
Qur'an admittedly still maintains the superiority of both father
and husband over a woman in the matter of marriage and divorce.
The latter, as emphasised by commentators, was personally
disapproved of by Mohammed, and was maintained by him to be
something "odious in the sight of God" (more on this subject
later). May we be allowed one further general comment that
might helpfully show something of the real tension in this subject.

> "[Mohammed's] own family life at Medina and his
> numerous marriages have been the subject of much in-
> sinuating comment on the one side and of heated and
> disingenuous apology on the other. The traditions make
> no secret of the attraction which he felt towards women,
> or of the fact that it was combined with a peculiarly strict
> regard for the proprieties. But critics have tended to
> overlook the almost unfailing patience which he dis-
> played even under provocation and the gentleness with
> which he attended to the griefs of all sorts of women and
> comforted them, even at times to the extent of revising his
> legislation."
> (Gibb 1979: 23)

Where did the improvement actually lie? It is to be found in the fact that from this time a woman was accepted as an individual in her own right instead of her being considered merely an object to be used. Does this sound strange to you? It is surely at this very point that we have problems as we look at the place of women in Islam! Are Muslims trying to whitewash their own dilemma? Listen to one protagonist:

> ". . . the most important legal enactments and general reform pronouncements of the Qur'an have been on the subjects of women and slavery. The Qur'an immensely improved the status of the woman in several directions but the most basic is the fact that the woman was given a fully-fledged personality. The spouses are declared to be each other's 'garments': the woman has been granted the same rights over man as man has over his wife, except that man, being the earning partner, is a degree higher. Unlimited polygamy was strictly regulated and the number of wives was limited to four, with the rider that if a husband feared that he could not do justice among several wives, he must marry only one wife. To this was added a general principle that 'you shall never be able to do justice among several wives no matter how desirous you are (to do so)'. The overall logical consequence of these pronouncements is a banning of polygamy under normal circumstances. Yet as an already existing institution polygamy was accepted on a legal plane, with the obvious guiding lines that when gradually social circumstances became more favourable, monogamy might be introduced. This is because no reformer who means to be effective can neglect the real situation and simply issue visionary statements. But the later Muslims did not watch the guiding lines of the Qur'an and, in fact, thwarted its intentions."   (Rahman 1979: 38)

Even though we may think some of these statements may be

questionable, or perhaps altogether too optimistic, the writer has
certainly made an interesting case. How valid is it?

When we refer to the teaching of the Qur'an on the place of
women, then we quickly discover that there are some very strong
sentiments expressed. As suggested above some of the ideas
became mellowed in Mohammed's thinking in later years. Let us
look at the situation as it is presented:

> "If any of your women commit fornication, call in four
> witnesses from among yourselves against them; if they
> testify of their guilt confine them to their houses till death
> overtakes them or till Allah finds another way for them."
>   (Qur'an Sura 4: 15)
> "Believers, it is unlawful for you to inherit the women
> of your deceased kinsmen against their will, or to bar them
> from remarrying, in order that you may force them to give
> up a part of what you have given them, unless they be
> guilty of a proven crime. Treat them with kindness; for
> even if you do not love them, it may well be that you may
> dislike a thing which Allah has meant for your own good.
> If you wish to divorce a woman in order to wed another,
> do not take from her the dowry you have given her even
> if it be a talent of gold. That would be improper and
> grossly unjust; for how can you take it back when you
> have lain with each other and entered into a firm contract?
> Henceforth you shall not marry the women who were
> married to your fathers. This was an evil practice, inde-
> cent and abominable." (Here follows a lengthy statement
> forbidding incest in various forms)
>   (Qur'an Sura 4: 19-22(-23))
> "If you fear a breach between a man and his wife,
> appoint an arbiter from his people and another from hers.
> If they wish to be reconciled Allah will bring them
> together again. Allah is wise and all-knowing."
>   (Qur'an Sura 4: 34-35)
> "Lawful to you are the believing women and the free

women from among those who were given the Scriptures
before you, provided that you give them their dowries and
live in honour with them, neither committing fornication
nor taking them as mistresses."   (Qur'an Sura 5: 5)

"Enjoin believing women to turn their eyes away from
temptation and to preserve their chastity; to cover their
adornments (except such as are normally displayed); to
draw their veils over their bosoms and not to reveal their
finery except to their husbands, their fathers, their
husband's fathers, their sons, their step-sons, their brothers, their brothers' sons, their sisters' sons, their women-
servants, and their slave-girls; male attendants lacking in
natural vigour, and children who have no carnal knowledge of women. And let them not stamp their feet in
walking so as to reveal their hidden trinkets."

(Qur'an Sura 24: 31)

On the whole we see here a genuine concern for propriety with
respect to the place of women in Muslim society at the time of
Mohammed. It is coloured by the prevailing situation. Mohammed was very aware of the abuse of women and was seeking to
bring about specific changes that would enhance their role and
command more respect for them. This is also balanced by a desire
to ensure that women knew their place in society, and lived
respectfully in that society without vaunting themselves. The
discerning Christian is surely reminded here of the teaching of
Paul on the way women, whether young, older or widowed, ought
to adopt modest and appropriate conduct: 1 Timothy 5:3-16;
Titus 2:3-5 (not at all forgetting that Paul equally applies himself
to the way men are to conduct themselves; we must keep
everything in balance here).

This is not to gloss over the fact that we see a number of major
problems with the way Muslims treat their women. They are not
considered to have equal rights, e.g. in divorce, and the expres-
sions used in the Qur'an give rise to real abuse. Let us further note
another reference in the Qur'an:

"Men have authority over women because Allah has made the one superior to the other, and because they spend their wealth to maintain them. Good women are obedient. They guard their unseen parts because Allah has guarded them. As for those from whom you fear disobedience, admonish them and send them to beds apart and beat them. Then if they obey you, take no further action against them. Allah is high, supreme."   (Qur'an Sura 4: 34)

Here we identify something of the harshness and the injustice that we so readily associate with the Muslim view of women. We have to face the difficulty that Muslims are allowed on religious grounds to have up to four wives at one time. However, the Qur'an clearly affirms that wives must be treated with deference, kindness and strict impartiality, and that if a man cannot treat all alike then he must keep to one! That is quite an admonition! In reality a man often only takes one wife for economic reasons: he finds that one is enough to be able to cope with! This helps to alleviate some of the abuses that we so readily identify in Islam.

As we continue to pursue this subject let us take a more specific look at some identifiable problem areas that face women in Islam.

3. Areas of Difficulty

We shall discuss three specific problem areas with respect to women in Islam. Though we divide them into distinctive subdivisions, it must be recognised that they are interdependent topics.

i) *Women's role in society*
Above all, in Islam women are considered as home-makers and the bearers of children. Their role in society is constrained by this view. Traditionally, education for women has been considered somewhat unwarranted and superfluous. Their skills were to be in keeping house! However, even this view has changed somewhat in recent years. For a daughter to have the

opportunity to receive a good education (even to degree level, if possible) is now often regarded as a considerable advantage, as this raises her status, acceptability, and attractiveness as a prospective wife! She is thus less of a liability, more of an asset, and this enhances the likelihood that she may be married-off well, and bring in a good dowry!

Her place in society varies considerably, depending somewhat in which Muslim country she is residing. She has far more opportunities to go to work in a country such as Turkey, but such a 'liberal and dangerous' practice is definitely felt to be out of place in other more fundamentalist countries. It must be recognised therefore that there is no general uniformity in the way women are considered and treated, only a prevailing atmosphere. In other words we are warned here to take each situation we meet on its own merits and we must learn the attitudes expressed within it.

Generally, of course, we meet with the problem of "*Purdah*". In most orthodox Muslim communities this principle is maintained with some variation. Basically, the concept is one of restriction of movement and confinement to homelife. The word literally means 'veil', or 'curtain', and refers to the way that women in the home are to keep themselves restricted to their area of the dwelling, behind the dividing curtain of the Bedouin tent, and the way this principle has been extended to more substantial property. Muslim propriety demands that women may not be seen by any man who could legally marry them.

Seclusion for Muslim women is not absolute in the sense that it would be for a western woman living in a nuclear family unit. Muslims maintain the joint family system, often described as the extended family unit, where the family home will consist of several houses together in one family compound. In that situation a wife is often freely allowed to move among the separate dwelling places in the family compound, as long as no male stranger is present. To move outside the confines of the family compound means that she must put on the '*burqah*', the black veil that covers her from head to toe, having slits for the eyes, or a net sewn into the veil through which to view the world. The Qur'anic justification of this is Sura 24: 31 (quoted above). The veil is often referred to by Christians in the west as demonstrating the bondage that Muslim women are in.

Why is such a custom so strenuously maintained? There are in fact some very interesting reasons for it. Its fundamental intention is for protection: to protect women from the lustful stares of men. Insistence on the veil being worn is considered to be an expression of love and respect by the husband. No self-respecting man would ever allow his wife to be degraded by the carnal and lascivious looks of other men. The veil is a symbol of her protection and security; a sign of her chastity and good reputation.

It must also be recognised that the Muslim woman herself would consider that she had sinned if she had ever caused a man to look upon her in such a way that would beguile him. She is ever seeking to be modest, not to mislead, nor to give any false impression of unseemly conduct. On the whole Muslim women accept this, and quite happily exercise the role of modest and submissive wife and mother. A Muslim wife knows that her responsibility is towards, and also lies within, her home. In recent years there has been some indication in places which have experienced a fundamentalist Islamic revolution, that many women have gone back to wearing the veil, and appear to have done so quite voluntarily for the most part. How can this be explained except in the terms already outlined?

Our outlook as western Christians has been to accuse Islam of imposing an extreme and unwarranted modesty and subjection on women. From our western perspective it appears to have been accomplished with real violence to an individual's rights and through intense pressures brought to bear. But a pertinent question to ask is: 'How do Muslim women view women in the West?' To reverse the question like this is very interesting and significant. Muslim women generally are totally shocked at how western, so-called Christian, women behave. They believe that western men cannot possibly value, respect or love their wives! They consider that the way western women dress in public is

utterly immodest, and no better than being in such a state of
undress as to cause men to desire and lust after them! Western
styles of fashion are thought to be a form of obscene and open
immorality! We would do well to reflect on this. There are some
good and valid reasons why Muslim women live as they do, and
we have much to lament as to how women are treated in our own
cultural situation, yes, and even within the Christian family.
Listen to one Muslim women's view as published in a leading
secular magazine in an Asian country:

> "In Pakistan men still are, as you call it, 'the boss'. And
> these men prefer to guard their women from the covetous
> eyes of the world. You may have the idea that the
> Pakistani woman leads a frightful life. Shrouded in
> anonymity, subservient, silent, humble. Please allow me
> to correct that impression. In public she appears to be all
> these things. But in the home she is revered. The veil she
> wears is both her prison and her pedestal. Because she
> works hard to please only her family, her husband does
> everything within his emotional and economic power to
> please her. He has pride in her. She is good because she
> is a woman and a bearer of his children. And she is
> precious because she is all his. Here is, in its way, a much
> easier life than that of the Western woman. Her position
> is crystal clear. Her husband is the boss, but in a very real
> spiritual way (the spirit is almost tangible in our lands) she
> rules."

(quoted in Bangladesh at a Glance 1980: 57)

A Muslim woman often does not feel as put down and under
such 'bondage' as western women would project. Every individual must be considered in each circumstance that we meet, and we
must listen to the woman's own views and understanding of the
matter. To do otherwise is not only the height of folly, but also
may well be a point of alienation. A Muslim woman delights to
conform to that pattern of life which will please her husband.

Desirable characteristics in a good Muslim woman are understood to include (a) modesty, (b) submissiveness, (c) readiness to
serve others, (d) a slow and graceful walk with small steps, and
(e) talking and laughing in a subdued and reserved way. In these
she may even be an enviable contrast to her male counterpart in
the family!

ii) *Women's role in marriage*

We have, of course, already demonstrated much of the
Muslim understanding of this aspect of the life of a Muslim
woman in the previous section. She is to be submissive to her
husband, and to work faithfully in the home, seeking to bring up
the children to the best of her ability. The officially permitted
polygamy is a great problem where it is encountered, but in a
great number of Muslim marriages it is no issue at all, owing to
social, economic, and practical circumstances. Many Muslim
marriages are happy marriages of one partner, where there is
mutual respect and a deepening love relationship. As is the
custom in the East, marriages are usually arranged; but this factor
alone does not diminish the prospects of their being successful
(we ought to remember that Isaac's marriage was arranged for
him!). In any culture it must be recognised that marriage has to
be worked at to make it successful. Muslim marriage is no
different in this respect. Children of an arranged marriage can
equally be born in love as in any western style marriage.

The extended family, found in most, if not all, Muslim
cultures is also a very important factor. The wife is not left to do
all the family chores on her own, nor is she left to look after the
children all by herself. The grandparents' role, and that of
mother-in-law, is very important in the extended family in
alleviating what western women can find to be excessive pressures in having to cope with keeping a home together. There is
often a greater measure of security, and a deeper sense of
solidarity.

Muslims are criticised for very good reason in that Islam
gives a woman a very low status. Over and against this there must

be a recognition of the strengths of the Muslim viewpoint. We can note four specific areas where there are real benefits for Muslim women:

> "a. All Muslim women have the opportunity to be married.
>
> b. Ideally, these marriages are arranged by concerned parents or other relatives.
>
> c. Compared to the West, the divorce rate, in most Muslim countries, is extremely low. There is security in marriage.
>
> d. The family becomes a supportive unit that acts as a refuge from the harsh realities of life."
>
> (Parshall 1980: 69)

It is right to state that there are some very bad attitudes among Muslim men regarding women and marriage. We may not be quite so ready to confess with shame that there are also some very bad attitudes among western men regarding women and marriage. Our task as Christians is to seek so to live to the glory and honour of God that we may show what the rightful place and role of women is in marriage by the practical demonstration of the love, respect, and consideration that we have for our own wives. We are enabled to do so by the strength and ability we receive through the Lord Jesus Christ, applied to our hearts by the Holy Spirit, and so bringing glory to the Father who decreed marriage to be a reflection of the mutual love the Father and the Son share together. We must also endeavour to have a much more careful and respectful attitude to women generally, in the light of the teaching of the Scriptures, as we learn the principles from both Old and New Testaments.

iii) *Women's rights in divorce*

Religious Muslim divorce, which governs all secular legislation, if any, in a Muslim country, is a comparatively easy affair. All the husband has to do is to say "Talaq, talaq, talaq," which is the Arabic for "I divorce you" three times over. There should then be a three month waiting period, to ascertain that the wife is not pregnant, before the divorce becomes final. Although this marital bond can be so easily dissolved by the husband, the wife has no similar right to divorce. However, Islam does teach that divorce is the most hateful to God of all the things that He permits. It is therefore something that is not to be undertaken rashly. The rationale of this somewhat questionable state of affairs is presented in a quotation given by Kenneth Cragg; a statement that will quickly be labelled 'chauvinistic' by many in our 'enlightened' day:

> "Since the man is sounder in judgement, and more capable of self-control and the one who has to pay the alimony, Islam has given him the right to dissolve marriage. Yet he is admonished not to divorce unless it is absolutely necessary, for that is hateful to Allah, and a good Muslim would not want to displease Him. The woman is liable to abuse such a right since she is temperamental and emotionally unstable. . . Yet Islam has permitted the woman, on concluding wedlock, to ask that the matter of divorce be the same for her as for the man. Furthermore the woman is permitted to seek a *qadi* to help her divorce, if the man has mistreated her or been too miserly."
>
> (Cragg 1956: 168)

That sentiment is likely to stir up the emotions! Not every Muslim would agree with its assessment either! The good news is that there is a family solidarity which checks the ease with which divorce can be obtained. Family pressure is often brought to bear where a problem is experienced, and marital problems can often be sorted out, given tact and common sense. Divorce can still be a real disgrace to the family name. In spite of appearances, the divorce rate in the Muslim world is estimated to be somewhat less than 10%, compared to our western world's figure of some 3 to 4 times higher that that. The current situation among those who would claim to be within the evangelical Christian

community should also make many of us consider carefully
before we are too ready to condemn others. Both the acceptability
and the seeking of divorce is on the increase: many Christians
appear to feel that easier divorce is more tolerable than the
problem of learning to overcome and work out marital problems
in the strength the Lord gives. There is also the dilemma of the
marriage where partners live together under sufferance,
unwilling to admit their problems even to themselves: such a
situation is also dishonouring to the Lord. We have little
foundation on which to 'cast stones' against Muslim family life,
without showing up our own faults and failures. We must remind
ourselves of the instructions that are clearly given us in Scripture
on the matter of making judgements: Romans 2:1-4. The Lord
Jesus Christ explicitly told us to examine ourselves and our own
motives when we see faults in others:

> **"Judge not that you be not judged. For with what
> judgment you judge, you will be judged; and
> with the same measure you use, it will be
> measures back to you."**   Matthew 7:1-2

Nor must we ignore what is surely another important matter
that has wider implications: namely, the way we conduct ourselves in mixed company: have we not become much too flippant
and careless in the respect and consideration with which we ought
to treat one another both in church life and in the world? Our
Muslim friends see great danger in our free and easy approach to
general relationships. Here is perhaps one reason why there is so
much breakdown of marriage relationships among Christians.
We need to take stock of ourselves. We surely need to repent of
our own sinfulness in the way we so lightly consider relationships
with the opposite sex, both in and out of marriage.

4. Our concern to reach women

Even as we consider this very sensitive issue, we have in mind that we do so because we are burdened to carry out the commission of our Lord Jesus Christ in presenting the gospel to Muslim women. We need to bear in mind a number of different factors that will help us do so. We need to be aware of those things that may give us the opportunity we look for. But we also have to admit that this is a very difficult task to undertake wisely and sensitively.

i) The first point to be made, and which must not be ignored or thought irrelevant, is that in seeking to share Christ with Muslims we must *take care that we witness only to members of our own sex*. As must surely have come across in the previous discussion Muslim men have a very strange view of western women, and consider them to be loose and easy. Because of their cultural norms they are immediately flattered by the attention of a western woman, and their motives in talking with you will at best be mixed. I strongly advocate that men only seek to witness to Muslim men, and women to endeavour to seek the opportunity to speak to Muslim women, who may often have to remain in the confines of their home. Ladies who have this burden to take the gospel to Muslim women should therefore take great care how they approach a Muslim man they may perhaps meet at the door of a house at which they are calling, not to enter into discussion with him, but respectfully request that they may speak to the ladies of that house.

N.B.: From this point on, all that is said will be relevant to the Christian woman who is seeking to witness to Muslim ladies. Male readers are invited to read on, as the principles may still equally apply to their own relationships to the menfolk. We all needs to be aware of the general situation we face when speaking to Muslims of Christ.

ii) The next point to bear in mind is that you *must be careful in your personal attitude about Muslim cultural norms*. It does not matter whether you disagree strongly about how you think Muslim women are being treated, or whether you feel you can tolerate Muslim attitudes, but you must take great care to show deference and respect to the way relationships are being treated in that particular household. Not to do so will alienate you from the male members of that house and, strange as it may seem to you, you may well offend the very women that you want to relate to. It may also have even further repercussions out into the rest of the Muslim community. We would also do well to consider the family as a whole, and seek to reach the elders or heads of the family wherever possible. This is the resposibility of Christian men. The possibility of such a head of family coming to faith in Christ would be, in human terms, a tremendous advantage. This would be seen in being able to share Christ with the other members of that particular family, without the exceedingly grievous threat of one who comes to believe in Christ as Saviour being unceremoniously thrown out of the family, or even, in some cases, coming under the threat of murder. Our Lord did not tell us to **"be wise as serpents and harmless as doves"** (Matthew 10:16) for no reason!

Another factor in reaching Muslim wives that may have to be borne in mind is the degree to which they feel responsible to their own families. In the experience of the author, it is possible that a wife may take her lead in religious teaching and understanding from her father, and not so much her husband. In some circumstances it has been known for the woman's father to cause a fuss on his daughter's behalf when it is considered that she is being neglected, mistreated, or misled. Thus to discover, for example, that the husband has turned away from Islam is enough for a wife's father to make a protest and seek to protect his daughter from being led astray. This has overtones on our understanding of a Muslim wife's allegiance in the domain of religious belief. We must not think only in simplistic terms of witness on a one-to-one basis with a Muslim woman as having no significant repercussions on the rest of the family. The very opposite is true, and therefore we would do well to make progress very carefully, thoughtfully, and with the wisdom that can only be given to us by the Holy Spirit.

iii) *Assess the situation that the Muslim woman herself faces.*
Here in the West a number of factors may have already altered
their circumstances so that it may differ somewhat from certain
details we have mentioned. Secularisation of immigrant families
takes place here in Britain, and gives the women of some Muslim
families much greater freedom of movement and expression.
The conditions under which many Muslim women live may not
be as 'bad' as your cultural prejudices may have lead you to
believe!

iv) *Befriend the ladies of the household and share your life
with them as far as possible*, through your common interests and
such practical skills as cooking and sewing. These things help to
bridge their natural reserve, and give you a platform on which to
base your friendship. Through mutual respect and trust you may
find that the Lord gives you the opportunity to ask about their
faith and to share with them something of yours. Remember that
these principles of sharing Christ have previously been covered
more fully in chapters 9 and 10.

****

It is our prayer that this discussion on the place and role of
women in Islam will be received in the same concerned attitude
as it is written. The author is only too painfully aware of the
prejudices, fixed views, and heated debate on the role of women
in Christian circles, apart from the problems that the subject of
'women in Islam' poses. It was not intended that personal
strongly held opinions, biases, or presuppositions be debated
here, but rather that we may take a serious look, with an open
mind, at the situation as it actually presents itself in practice.

Postscript: The subject of the family is also of great interest
and relevance but outside the scope of this study. However the
author is somewhat disturbed about one recent comment heard in

the area of our concern to reach Muslims with the gospel. This was to the effect that as the children of Muslim families are more open to our own cultural influences we should devote our efforts in reaching them rather than their parents. The impression given was that the children would be more readily influenced by the gospel message, and more likely to overthrow their family cultural norms. In effect this approach is an attempt to bypass some of the ingrained Islamic principles of the parents in an attempt to reach the more vulnerable members of the family. This approach in reality means that the family unit is not being respected, and nothing worse can be designed to bring down the ire of the Muslim community on us than this. The author would strongly recommend that we respect Muslim views, beliefs and practices, *especially* at family level. This must be kept in the right perspective: to respect Muslim culture and practice *does not* mean that we condone or agree with them, nor does it mean that we do not wish to see their attitudes and understanding change as the light of the gospel dawns in their hearts through the application of saving grace by the power of the Holy Spirit. We ought, however, to avoid doing *anything* that may alienate Muslims from us. To employ such a method as the one proposed would very quickly achieve that result! Rather we must come to the Muslim family with the love of the Lord Jesus Christ which was expressed in respect, concern, compassion, tenderness, and appreciation for the weaknesses of those for whom He had come to give His life as "*a ransom for many*".

> "By this we know love, because He laid down His life for us. And we also ought to lay down our lives for the brethren... My little children, let us not love in word or in tongue, but in deed and in truth... And this is His commandment: that we should believe on the name of His Son Jesus Christ and love one another, as He gave us commandment."   1 John 3:16,18,23

BIBLIOGRAPHY

Please note that very few of the following books have been written from the perspective of the doctrines of grace. Therefore, they have to be read with discernment. This does not mean that they are not worthy of our attention: rather, the opposite is true. These books present valuable information or important questions that we must face. We should consider such material together with an open Bible, and with spiritual perceptiveness. We can take care to sift out those ideas and propositions that are not helpful to a faithful presentation of the gospel of sovereign grace to people of Islamic persuasion.

Bangladesh at a Glance. Chittagong: A.B.W.E., 1980

'Banner of Truth' Magazine, Issue 266. Banner of Truth Trust, November, 1985.

BUDD, Jack. *Islam Teach In: 'How to Witness to Muslims'*. Red Sea Mission Team, N.D.

BUDD, Jack. *Studies on Islam: 'A Simple Outline of the Islamic Faith'*. Red Sea Mission Team, 1973

* CHAPMAN, C. *"You Go And Do The Same"*. Church Missionary Society/ BMMF International, 1983.

CHRISTENSEN, Jens. *The Practical Approach to Muslims*. The North Africa Mission, 1977

* *Christian Witness Among Muslims*. Africa Christian Press, 1971.

* COOPER, Anne. *Ishmael, My Brother*. MARC/STL Books, 1985.

* CRAGG, Kenneth. *The Call of the Minaret*. New York: Oxford University Press, 1956.

ELDER, J. *The Biblical Approach to the Muslim*. Leadership Instruction and Training International, N.D.

GIBB, H. A. R. *Islam*. Hyderabad: Henry Martyn Institute of Islamic Studies, 1979 (London: Oxford University Press, 1969 [1949])

GOLDSMITH, Martin. *Islam and Christian Witness*. Hodder and Stoughton, 1982.

GUILLAUME, Alfred. *Islam*. Penguin Books Ltd., 1977 (1954)

HAQQ, Abdiyah A. A. *Sharing Your Faith with a Muslim*. Bethany Fellowship, 1980.

HARRIS, G. K. *How To Lead Moslems To Christ*. China Inland Mission, 1957.

* HOUGHTON, S. M. *Sketches from Church History*. Banner of Truth Trust, 1980.

JONES, L. Bevan. *The People of the Mosque*. Delhi: ISPCK./ Madras: Christian Literature Society, 1980 (First edition 1932)

* KARIM, Prof. M. N. *"Hajj and Muslim Fraternity"*. Bangladesh Observer, 27th September, 1982.

MADAMY, Bassam M. *Sharing God's Word With A Muslim*. The Back to God Hour Publications, 1981.

MARSH, C. R. *Share Your Faith With A Muslim*. Moody Press, 1975.

* MAWDUDI, Abul A'la. *Towards Understanding Islam*. Islamic Foundation, 1981.

McCURRY, Don M. (Editor) *The Gospel and Islam*. MARC., 1979.

* MUSLEHUDDIN, Mohammad. *Sociology and Islam*. Lahore: Islamic Publications, 1977.

PARRINDER, Geoffrey. *Jesus in the Qur'an*. Faber and Faber, 1965

PARSHALL, Phil. *Beyond the Mosque*. Baker Book House, 1985.

PARSHALL, Phil. *Bridges to Islam*. Baker Book House, 1983.

PARSHALL, Phil. *New Paths in Muslim Evangelism*. Baker Book House, 1980.

PARSHALL, Phil. *The Fortress and the Fire*. Bombay: Gospel Literature Service, 1976.

* QUR'AN: The only authoritative edition is considered to be the Arabic, according to the Muslim. The following English renderings have been quoted in this book. Quotations have been taken from Dawood unless otherwise stated.
ARBERRY, A. J. *The Koran Interpreted.* Macmillan Publishing Co., Inc., 1955.
DAWOOD, N. J. *The Koran.* Penguin Books, 1956.
PICKTHALL, Mohammed M. *The Meaning of the Glorious Koran.* Mentor Book (New American Library, Inc.), N.D.
RAHMAN, Fazlur. *Islam.* University of Chicago Press, 1979 (1966)
Reaching Muslims Today. North Africa Mission, 1976.
RODINSON, Maxime. *Mohammed.* Penguin Books Ltd., 1976 (1972)
* SHENK, David W. "The Muslim Umma and the Growth of the Church", *Exploring Church Growth,* Edited by Wilbert R. Shenk. Wm. B. Eerdmans Publishing Company, 1983.
SPENCER, H. *Islam And The Gospel Of God.* Delhi: ISPCK., 1956.
ST. CLAIR-TISDALL. *The Sources of Islam.* Edinburgh: T. & T. Clark, reprinted by Birmingham Bible Institute Press, N.D.
STACEY, Vivienne. *Practical Lessons for Evangelism Among Muslims.* Wiesbaden: Orientdienst eV., N.D.
STANTON, H.U. Weitbrecht. *The Teaching of the Qur'an.* SPCK., 1969.
WATT, W. Montgomery. *Muhammad: Prophet and Statesman.* Oxford University Press, 1980 (1961)
* WE BELIEVE: *The Baptist Affirmation of Faith 1966 and A Guide to Church Fellowship.* Grace Baptist Assembly (Grace Publications Trust), 1983 (1966,1974)

*These sources are directly quoted in the text.

Appendix 1
The Ninety-nine Names of God

1.	Ar Rahman	The Compassionate
2.	Ar Rahim	The Merciful
3.	Al Malik	The King
4.	Al Quddus	The Holy One
5.	As Salam	The Peace
6.	Al Mu'min	The Faithful One
7.	Al Muhaimin	The Protector
8.	Al 'Aziz	The Mighty
9.	Al Jabbar	The Almighty
10.	Al Mutakabbir	The Great One
11.	Al Khaliq	The Creator
12.	Al Bari	The Maker
13.	Al Musawwir	The Fashioner
14.	Al Ghaffar	The One Who Forgives
15.	Al Qahhar	The Dominant
16.	Al Wahhab	The Bestower
17.	Ar Razzaq	The Provider, the Bestower of Daily Bread
18.	Al Fattah	The Opener
19.	Al 'Alim	The All Knowing
20.	Al Qabiz	The Restrainer
21.	Al Basit	The Expander
22.	Al Khafiz	The One Who Humbles
23.	Ar Rafi'	The One Who Exalts
24.	Al Mu'izz	The One Who Honours
25.	Al Muzil	The Destroyer
26.	As Sami'	The One Who Hears
27.	Al Basir	The One Who Sees

28.	Al Hakam	The Ruler/Judge
29.	Al 'Adl	The Just
30.	Al Latif	The Gracious
31.	Al Khabir	The Aware
32.	Al Halim	The Merciful (Forbearing)
33.	Al 'Adhim	The Great One
34.	Al Ghafur	The One Who Pardons
35.	Ash Shakur	The Rewarder
36.	Al 'Ali	The Most High
37.	Al Kabir	The Great Lord
38.	Al Hafiz	The Guardian
39.	Al Muqit	The Giver of Strength
40.	Al Hasib	The Reckoner
41.	Al Jalil	The Majestic, All-glorious
42.	Al Karim	The Bountiful
43.	Ar Raqib	The Watcher
44.	Al Mujib	The One who Hears Prayer
45.	Al Wasi'	The Comprehensive
46.	Al Hakim	The Wise Physician
47.	Al Wudud	The All-Loving
48.	Al Majid	The Glorious
49.	Al Baith	The Awakener
50.	Ash Shahid	The Witness
51.	Al Haqq	The Truth
52.	Al Wakil	The Guardian
53.	Al Qawi	The Powerful
54.	Al Matin	The Firm
55.	Al Wali	The Nearest Friend
56.	Al Hamid	The Praiseworthy
57.	Al Muhsi	The Enumerator
58.	Al Mubdi	The First Cause
59.	Al Mu'id	The Restorer
60.	Al Muhyi	The Life-giver
61.	Al Mumit	The Death-giver
62.	Al Haiy	The Living
63.	Al Qaiyum	The Self-Subsisting

64.	Al Wajid	The One Who Finds
65.	Al Majid	The Magnificent
66.	Al Wahid	The One (Unique)
67.	As Samad	The Eternal
68.	Al Qadir	The Powerful
69.	Al Muqtadir	The Prevailing
70.	Al Muqaddim	The One Who Brings Forward
71.	Al Mu'akhkhir	The One Who Defers
72.	Al Awwal	The First
73.	Al Akhir	The Last
74.	Al Tahir	The Evident
75.	Al Batin	The Hidden
76.	Al Wali	The Governor
77.	Al Muta'ali	The Exalted (Sublime)
78.	Al Barr	The Righteous
79.	At Tauwab	The Accepter of Repentance, (The Propitious)
80.	Al Muntaqim	The Avenger
81.	Al 'Afuw	The Pardoner
82.	Ar Ra'uf	The One Who Blesses
83.	Malik al Mulk	The Ruler of the Kingdom (The King of Kingdoms)
84.	Dhu al Jalali wa al Ikram	The Lord of Glory and Honour
85.	Al Muqsit	The Impartial One
86.	Al Jami'	The Assembler
87.	Al Ghani	The Independent and Rich
88.	Al Mughni	The Enricher
89.	Al Mu'ti	The Giver
90.	Al Mani'	The Withholder
91.	Adh Dharr	The Afflicter
92.	An Nafi'	The Benefactor
93.	An Nur	The Light
94.	Al Hadi	The Guide
95.	Al Badi'	The Incomparable
96.	Al Baqi	The One Who Remains

95.	Al Warith	The Inheritor
98.	Ar Rashid	The Director
99.	As Sabur	The Patient One

The above list is a composite one derived from various sources. Some authorities like to include a hundredth name, perhaps substituting "*Allah*". Others believe that this name is hidden with God, that only He knows it, and can reveal it. It is often referred to as "*Ism al A'dham*", 'the Exalted Name' which no human being knows.

The names are commonly classified by dividing them into two groups that define the attributes: (i) "*asmau'l-jalaliya*", the 'terrible' attributes; and (ii) "*Asmau'l-jamaliya*", the 'glorious' attributes. Bevan Jones gives a more detailed summary analysis of the names used:

i.   Seven describe Allah's Oneness and Absolute Being.
ii.   Five speak of Him as Creator, or Originator of all nature.
iii.   Twenty-four show Him as merciful and gracious (i.e., to believers!). These are also called 'beautiful' names and are some of the most often used in the Qur'an.
iv.   Thirty-six emphasise Allah's power and pride and absolute sovereignty: the 'terrible' attributes.
v.   Five reveal Him as hurting and avenging. In Muslim terms, He is a God who leads astray, avenges, withholds His mercies, and works harm (cf. Qur'an: Sura 6:39, 32:21, 13:32, 45:23).
vi.   Four refer particularly to the moral qualities in Allah.

Appendix 2
Comparison of Muslim and Christian World Views

The following is a representation of the differing viewpoints between Muslims and western Christians. A certain amount of difference has arisen because of the contrasting cultural backgrounds represented by 'East' and 'West'. But the differences are not merely cultural: the various doctrines have made a significant impact on both societies. As varied as the Muslim countries are, there is quite significant correspondence between them through the influence of Islamic doctrine.

Concept	Muslim	Western Christian
1. Unity	Basic to every aspect of life.	Considered important only if it appears reasonable.
2. Time	Great respect for the past and tradition. Generally regarded in indefinite terms: the event is more important.	Emphasis towards the future. Past is outdated: the future is considered a challenge.
3. Family	Solidarity of the extended family. Family responsibility is considered a major priority.	Emphasis placed more on the rights of the individual in society. (Biblical Christianity however teaches solidarity of the family unit and responsibility of relationship.)

4. Peace	Idea of harmony, health and integration. = Total way of life. Look for both subjective and external objective expression.	Idea of harmony and contentment. = One aspect of life. Emphasis on subjective quality; often a more spiritual ideal.
5. Honour	All-important consideration. Maintaining family honour is a major priority.	Has importance for an individual; emphasis on being an honourable person.
6. Status in Society	Associated with birth, wealth, family name, and age (often overriding educational considerations).	Usually through some achievement, accomplished through personal hard work.
7. Individualism	Considered much less important than the group opinion, esp. in matters of welfare and decisions to be made.	Independent thinking is considered beneficial; strong personal decisions valued.
8. Secularism	A totally unacceptable trend within society; vital to uphold principle of theocracy. Islamic law is linked to national pride.	A largely acceptable trend; belief must be seen to be relevant to life. Often considered to co-exist with spiritual expression of life (but spiritually unhealthy!)
9. Change	Undesirable; causes identity crisis in community.	Usually valued and considered desirable; Looked on as synonymous with progress.

| 10. Equality | A highly valued but theoretical ideal of brotherhood of man which is rarely practised consistently. | Valued ideal, with practical breakdowns, and inconsistencies. |
| 11. Organisation | Very little concern shown for structured planning and method. | Considered an imperative for successful society and fulfilling life. |

Appendix 3

Comparison of Religious Terminology

Vocabulary	Muslim	Christian
1. God	Sovereign. Almighty. (Holy) Merciful. Unpredictable. Unknowable. Indifferent. - Distant.	Sovereign. Almighty. Holy. Loving & Merciful. Unchangeable. Concerned. Just. - Personal.
2. Jesus	Prophet. Sinless.	God. Perfect Man.
3. Trinity	God, Mary, Jesus (in terms of human relations).	Father, Son, Holy Spirit (In terms of spiritual relationship).
4. Bible	Revelation from God - changed, corrupted.	Final and complete revelation, fully inspired and totally infallible.
5. Word of God	- Qur'an. - Title of Jesus.	Holy Bible (written word). Person of Jesus (living Word).

6. Faith	Obedience to God's law.	Exercised as gift of God.
	Object of: God as revealed in the Qur'an (through Mohammed).	In Jesus as God
	Expressed in works.	Demonstrated through works.
7. Sin	Shame, embarrassment - feels guilt when caught!	Rebellion, disobedience - guilt is constant reality.
8. Salvation	Requirement: faith by works.	Requirement: repentance and faith, not works.
	Provider: God.	Provider: God in Christ.
	End: sensual paradise.	End: eternal life with Christ in glory (emphasis on the spiritual)
	No assurance.	Assurance granted.
9. Sanctification	Emphasis on obedience and ritual: a conforming to the will of God by works.	A continuing work of the Holy Spirit in the life of a believer, a gradual conforming to 'be like Christ'.
10. Works	Obedience to the laws of God seeking to win his favour; to obtain merit that will earn acceptance with and approval of God.	The grateful response to grace; the evidence of a changed life as thankful obedience for having received mercy and forgiveness. *Not* to win approval of God.

Appendices   143

11. Love	No concept of God of love. In human relationships: it is considered as the bond that unites the extended family; expressed as loyalty.	The motivating factor of the character of God, His nature, to grant mercy and forgiveness. A vital concept of love to God primarily, in response to His love, the motivating principle of life; to be extended in all human relationships; epitomised in christian fellowship. Love in the family is modelled on Christ's love for His people.
12. Supernatural	Belief in the spirit world; in angels. Superstition maintains animistic fears.	Belief based on biblical revelation. Spiritual relationships to be kept within a biblical framework. Love for God dispels all fear.
13. Grace	Inadequate concept: understood that Divine favour *must* be merited. No hope apart from works.	The free, undeserved, unmerited favour, goodness and mercy of the just and holy God to sinners. The basis of any meaningful relationship with God.